Chinese Macro-economy in the Process of Bottoming-Out and Rebounding

Authors: Liu Yuanchun, Yan Yan, Liu Xiaoguang

Paths International Ltd

中国社会科学出版社
CHINA SOCIAL SCIENCES PRESS

Abstract: Chinese economy continued slowing down in 2015, and the growth will be moderating in 2016. In the shadow of the global business cycle, China's real estate cycle, debt cycle, inventory cycle, new industrial breeding cycle and political cycle, Chinese economy will face severe headwinds in 2016. Meanwhile, a lot of new industries and new growth engines have been fostered in Chinese economy, making it a mixture of stagnancy and flourish. The basis of next round rapid growth is being built in the process of deepening adjustment. In the face of two main kinds of economic risks in 2016, high attention must be paid to the following issues: the reshape of the incentive system, the recovery of the real estate market, the evolvement of the world economy, and the re-orientation of the macro economic policy. The bottom of Chinese economy is expected to appear in the second half in 2016, and a steady rebound to be in late 2017, returning to the rapid growth track.

Key Words: Bottom and Rebound Macro economic Policy Policy Re-orientation

Contents

1. General Comments and Forecast

1.1. Review of the economic performance in 2015

2015 was a year in which the new normal state of the Chinese macro-economy entered into a new and difficult phase in an all-round way. It also marked a year in which Chinese macro-economy witnessed polarizing structures, deviating micro-performance and intensifying volatilities. The differences between 2015 and other years are:

1. Influenced by the shrinking of export and continuing decrease in investment growth rate, the slow-down of Chinese economy growth has been beyond expectation with various kinds of indicators coming down to the lowest point over the past 20 years. The GDP growth rate was below 7%; non-financial industries growth rate was below 6%; price value added to industries and main business income embraced "zero growth"; enterprise profits and government revenue had "minus growth"—all of these indicated that Chinese macro-economy stepped into a serious downturn period in 2015.

2. Influenced by factors such as imported deflation, insufficient effective demand and overcapacity, etc., the GDP deflator had reached the "negative growth section", which indicated that the main factors causing the Chinese economic downturn had turned from long-term ones with a trend into medium and short term periodic ones. The insufficient effective demand and overall prevalence of deflation had gradually became the core issues for macro-control. Continuous industrial depression began

to expand into service and consumption sectors, and macro-prosperity started to withstand the downturn pressure in all aspects.

3. The rapid growth of "recessionary trade surplus" caused by small-degree negative growth of export and large-degree negative growth of import not only indicated that there was redundant saving in Chinese macro economy, but also clarified that the decrease rate of domestic demand was far larger than that of demand abroad. The pressure of Chinese structural adjustment caused by global imbalance, as well as the distortion made by domestic imbalance, had became the leading factor for Chinese economic downturn. Structural rebalance should be one of the major missions in tackling total imbalance.

4. Influenced by the factors such as profits decrease, expectation setback and price drop, the capital turnover slowed down, social financing and bank loans came across endogenous shrink, and capital chain began to show abnormal changes. While the liquidity was much less able to permeate the real economy, "recessional bubble" continued to show up – for instance, the stock market roaring starting from the end of 2014 to the second quarter of 2015, the house price hike took place in first-tier cities since the April of 2015, and the prosperity we saw in debt market since the second quarter of the same year — all indicated that liquidity in China began to be stuck in a dilemma.

5. The idea of reducing leverage and debts by means such as equity financing and local debts was confronted with immense difficulties. The events such as "Tianwei Group debt default", " stock market crash of June 14th , "exchange rate panic of August 11th", and "Sinosteel Cooperation debt default" not only indicated that the financial risk level of China was up to a new high, but also proved that China needed more accuracy in adjustments on its economic structure. The monetary and financial policy were not only unable to reach their goals under current interest pattern and supervision system, but also became the new source and trigger to risks.

6. The effects of various kinds of countermeasures aiming to sustain economic growth had began to fade away in an acceleratory way. The existing policies, affected by factors such as laziness and unwillingness showed by some local governments when addressing issues, interest conflicts among different governmental sectors, restructuring of

government-business relations and transforming of encouragement motivation system, were hard to play their supposed roles. The macro-economy policy was facing with the risk of malfunction in all aspects. The financial policy which were designed to be positive were in fact not positive, the monetary policy which was made to be prudent was actually not prudent, and the industrial policy which ought to be expansive was not in place. All of these phenomenons, combined with the laches of elite class, formed the root cause responsible for the downturn of Chinese economy.

7. At the same time when all kinds of indexes were worsening, the micro-behaviour model of Chinese economy was at the brink of deviation as a whole.

From the perspective of enterprise, the "deflation-debt effect" was looming large. On one hand, the continuous fall of production price enormously undermined the ability to make profits possessed by main economic actors; on the other hand, the continuous rising debts led to the increasingly higher enterprise debt cost. The production actors in China, who secured new loans to pay off the old debts in the past, started to secure new loans to pay off the interest on their old debts. This directly led to overall prevalence of endogenous contract such as overall capital shrinking, investment decrease, accelerative reduction on number of unsold products and low expectation, etc.

From the perspective of government, under the pressure from the weakness of tax revenue and huge drop of land transfer expense, the decrease of government revenue growth rate was apparent. With difficulties in daily operations began to show up at some regional governments, as well as the laziness and unwillingness in government behaviours were normalized, the behaviour model of governments at various levels were stuck in a vacuum where the new encouragement and motivation mechanism was yet to replace the old one.

From the perspective of household, the income distribution policy and the stabilization maintaining policy ensured that household income did not drop together with the downturn of GDP growth rate. However, the continuous plummet of macro prosperity and abnormal fluctuation of capital prices directly led to lower income expectation and consumption confidence. Hence, the long-term prosperous situation of consumption also faced with downward pressure.

8. What was worth our close attention was a fact telling apart China's economic downturn at current stage from other rounds of economic downturn in the past and economic weakness in other emerging economies—polarization appeared in Chinese economic downturn, which featured the co-existence of prosperity seen in successfully transformed regions and depression seen in the regions that stuck in their transformation; prosperity in the field of consumption and depression in the field of production; emergence of new types of industries and confusion of traditional manufacturing; activeness of innovation areas and stagnation of labour-intensive industries. This polarization did not only indicate that the critical period for China to deeply adjust its economic structures, to release its risks in all aspects and to bottom out, was coming, but also meant that Chinese economy was harboring new vitality despite of its weak performance. We could already see the dawn light against the darkness of economic slow-down. With incessant process of bottoming out, Chinese economy began to lay a foundation for the next round of growth with medium and high speed.

9. The constant growth-sustain policy started to take effects in the fourth quarter of 2015 with many macro-economy indicators coming back to normal state. However, due to the lasting poor performance of external environment, the weakening of internal driving force for growth and various cyclic and long-term forces did not bottom out yet, the third and fourth quarter of 2015 were not the bottom for this round of economic growth.

1.2. Prospect of economic growth in 2016

In 2016, Chinese economy will keep on its way to bottom out. On one hand, many macro-economy indicators will further fall back; on the other hand, many micro-economy indicators might deviate in a all-round way. In that case, the deviation will make changes going beyond expectation on the depth of economic bottom and the time it takes to bottom out.

What we must clarify is that the bottom of this round of economic growth was a joint product of various kinds of periodic forces. Will the world economy bottom out for the second time in 2016? Will real estate investment successfully rise up again in the second quarter of 2016? Will China's debt restructuring reduce the debt burden on enterprises? Will China launch inventory adjustment in a large scale? Will incremental expansion be enough to cover the shortfall caused by imbalanced reversion and traditional inventory adjustments? Will the relocation of macro-economy policy be able to change pessimistic expectations made by micro-economic actors, and efficiently dissolve the overall explicitation of "deflation-debt effects"? Will the encouragement and motivation mechanism brought by the new round of reform and adjustment be established effectively? All the factors abovementioned will jointly determine the bottom of this round of Chinese economic growth, as well as its depth to the bottom and the time it takes to bottom out.

1. In 2016, the world economy will still be difficult to get rid of the downturn state we saw in 2015. First, because of the normalization of monetary policy of the U.S., the further plummet of China's import demand, the constant price drop of international bulk commodity and deep-level problems cause by the mismatch in global manufacture industries in earlier stages, in 2016 the volatilities faced by emerging economies will be larger than any other volatilities faced by these economies in the past. Second, the challenges beyond expectation posed by various kinds of geopolitics might sabotage the recovery of European economy. Third, due to the fact that global investment and trade decrease have not come to an end, the world macro-economy, which was in need of unified macro-economy policy and coordination, lacked the foundation for economic recovery and supports provided by mid-term prosperous fundamentals. Fourth, decided by the way in which the world crisis spreads, this round of crisis is still keep spreading from finance to real economy, from the core to the peripheral. The emerging economies have just started the work to adjust their balance sheet. Therefore, the world economy will not only face with overall and long-lasting slowdown, but also will be possible to bottom out for the second time. This conclusion means that China will not only be challenged by world trade decline, but also at the same time will be affected by global capital abnormality.

It will be very difficult for the Chinese economy to realize periodic reversion before the world economy bottoms out.

2. China has not started its inventory adjustments in a substantive way. The superfluous industrial capacities have not been eliminated as a whole. “Zombie enterprises” are still ubiquitous acting as capital black holes. State-owned enterprises with debt hangover are still the investment foci of various kind of capital affected by the snowball effect… therefore, the supply-side inventory adjustments which will be carried out in 2016 will determine the bottom of inventory and the time for reversion. The bottom of entire economy will not be reached until we see the bottom of inventory economy.

3. Too many houses held in reserve and excessive regional division determines that the cyclic adjustment of Chinese real estate industry will take more time compared with previous adjustments. In addition, the recovery risks a premature end. Although there is a strong uncertainty in the expectation on overall recovery of real estate in 2016, the upcoming inventory real estate policy will largely undermine this uncertainty, and will in advance realize the reversion of real estate investment growth rate. If the reversion did not happen, the short-term economic stability would have been difficult to be achieved.

4. Obvious accomplishments have been achieved in increment adjustment during recent years, but a relatively long period is needed to nurture new industries, new activities and new driving force. It is difficult to cover the gap brought by the transforming of traditional forces. The ever-increasing incremental adjustments in 2016 will face with restrictions of government spending on one hand, and bubble risk caused by excessive support from the government on the other hand.

5. The debt cycle is the most direct force that determines the cycle of Chinese economic growth in this round. The debt ratio increase has been enlarged by the stock market collapse took place between June and July of 2015. The situation of Chinese debt cycle will be decided directly by the overall restart of IPO projects in China, acceleration of local bond swap and reduction of non-performing assets. If the debt dilemma could be not solved and capital black holes not eliminated, the medium and high speed growth mechanism of Chinese economy would have been difficult to be in place.

6. The shortage of encouragement and motivation mechanism in the new round of large-scale reform and adjustment is the deep-level reason of constant economic downturn. Whether the relocation of large-scale reform and adjustment in 2016 will able to build up a new encouragement and motivation mechanism or not is a critical condition for Chinese economy to bottom out.

1.3. Macro-economic index forecast for 2015-2016

Base on the qualitative observations made in above passages, we can use the macro-economic analysis and forecast model proposed by the Renmin University—CMAFM Model, to set up a hypothesis on main macro-economic policies: (1) fiscal budget real deficit of 2015 was 1600 billion yuan and 2100 billion yuan; (2) the average exchange rate between RMB and US dollars in 2015 and 2016 is respectively 6.21:1 and 6.50:1. The forecast results of Chinese macro-economic situation in 2015 and 2016 is shown in table 1-1 :

Table 1-1: Macro-economic Predicators

Predictors	2014	2015 (Jan.–Sept.)	2015 (Prediction)	2016 (Prediction)
1. Growth rate of GDP(%)	7.3	6.9	6.9	6.6
Added value of the Primary industry	4.1	3.8	4.0	4.0
Added value of the secondary industry	7.3	6.0	5.9	5.4
Added value of the tertiary industry	7.8	8.4	8.2	8.0
2. Total asset investment in society (billion yuan)	50200.5	39453.1	55220.6	60521.8
(grwoth rate, %)	15.7	10.3	10.0	9.6
Total retail sales of social consumer goods (billion yuan)	26239.4	21608	29020.8	32009.9

(Contd.)

Predictors	2014	2015 (Jan.–Sept.)	2015 (Prediction)	2016 (Prediction)
(growth rate, %)	12.0	10.5	10.6	10.3
3. Export (billion yuan)	14391.2	10236.5	14204.1	14503
(growth rate, %)	4.9	-1.8	-1.3	2.1
Import (billion yuan)	12042.3	7633.4	10597.2	10713.8
(growth rate, %)	-0.6	-15.1	-12.0	1.1
4. Growth rate of M2 (%)	12.2	13.1	13.3	13.0
Total financing in society (billion yuan)	16460	11940	15192.6	16256.1
5. Growth rate of residence consumption price indictor (%)	2.1	1.4	1.4	1.3
Growth rate of GDP deflator (%)	0.8	-0.3	-0.5	-0.1
6. National governmental income (billion yuan)	19444.3	14157.8	19024.4	19423.7
Growth rate (%)	7.2	-2.6	-2.2	2.1
National general public budget income (billion yuan)	14035	11441.2	15129.7	16113.2
National government-controlled funds income (billion yuan)	54093	27166	38947	33105

1. Affected by various kinds of policies aiming to sustain economic growth, the rapidly downward economic growth in the first half of 2015 began to be stable in the fourth quarter of the year. However, due to the constant weakness of demand abroad and the amelioration of policy stimulus effects, the foundation for an increasingly stable economic situation is not solid. The general picture of macro-economy is still bleak. It is estimated that the real growth rate of GDP for the whole year will be 6.9%, a 0.4% decrease compared with the real growth rate in

2014. Although this number has basically complete the goal set up by the government, due to the fact that the GDP deflator is -0.5%, the nominal GDP growth rate is only 6.4%, and the nominal growth rate of industrial added value is only 0.2%, a 1.8% and 4.7% decrease compare with those in the year of 2014. The level of difficulty facing the general economic situation is higher than what is shown by the real growth.

2. From the perspective of supply-side, constantly influenced by the depressive industry, the extent of decrease in the send industry is enlarged, and the tertiary industry embraces a strong rebound against all adversities. It is estimated that the growth rate of the second industry in 2015 will be 5.9%, a 1.4 % decrease compared with that of 2014; the growth rate of the tertiary industry will in 2015 will be 8.2%, a 0.4% increase compared with that of 2014; the first industry, affected by various kinds of agriculture policies, remains relatively stable with the growth rate being 4.0%. There are something worth our attention: first, the price added value to the second industry (or nominal growth rate) is only 0.6%, and the main business income and profits all meet with "negative growth"; second, the major reason for the increase in the tertiary industry real growth is the rapid growth of financial sector, without which the growth rate of tertiary industry is only 6%, the real growth rate of GDP is only 6%, and the nominal growth rate of GDP is only 5.5%

3. From the perspective of the total demand, the three big demands all show signs of shrinking. Among them, the decrease in the growth rate of investment and export is relatively more prominent. The reasons are: first, the asset investment of whole society decreases continuously affected by the weakness of manufacturing and real estate industry investment. It is estimated that the asset investment growth rate is only 10%, a 5.7% decrease compared with that of 2014. Second, affected by global trade contract and domestic investment downturn, the export and import decrease dramatically. It is estimated that the growth rate of export will be -1.3% and -12%. This asymmetric downturn results in a trade surplus of 3606.9 billion yuan (580.8 billion US dollar, a 53.6% increase compared with that of 2014, with its share in GDP rising from 37% in 2014 to 53%. The widening of recessive surplus means that China's internal imbalance is worsening further. Third, the consumption

remains stable. It is estimated that the total social retail sales in 2015will increase by 10.6 % compared with that in 2014. The nominal growth rate of consumption decreases by 1.4% compared with that in 2014, but the real growth rate of consumption decreases by 0.8% if the factor of price is not taken into consideration.

4. Affected by various factors such as imbalance of supply-demand relation and imported inflation, etc., the price level in 2015 falls down in a noticeable way. It is estimated that the growth rate of CPI for the whole year will be 1.4%, a 0.6 % decrease compared with that of 2014. It is far below the policy target aiming to reach a growth rate at 3.0%. what are worth our attention are: (1) the GDP deflator of 2015 is minus, and the its growth rate for the whole year is -0.5%, a 1.3% decrease compared with that in 2014. (2) The deflation in industrial areas is worsening and likely to expand. The PPI in 2015 is -5.2%, a 3% decrease compared with that in 2014. (3) the service price and core CPI slightly drops down, making a 0,5% and 0.1% decrease compared with those in 2014.

5. The prudent monetary policy continues to be deployed. However, pressured by the endogenous capital shrinking, the gap between money supply and social financing is widening substantially, and the liquidity continues to be less able to permeate the real economy. It is estimated that the growth rate of M2 will be staying at 13.3%, total social financing will be 15192 .6 billion yuan with the growth rate being -7.7%. The conflict between increasing money supply and decreasing financing is further compounded.

6. Affected by recessive real estate, industry and import, it is estimated that the growth rate of Chinese government revenue will be -2.2%. There will be a overall larger pressure from public finance confronting China.

2016 will be the first year when Chinese economy continues to bottom out. It will also be the most difficult year over recent time. Various kinds of macro-economic indexes will further fall back, the micro-economic operation mechanism will have more deviations. This will bring an opportunity for China to implement substantial inventory adjustments, comprehensive supply-side reform and expansion on demand in a larger scale, which will lay a foundation for the reversion of economic cycle as well as medium and high speed economic growth in 2017.

1. it is estimated that the real growth rate of GDP in 2016 will be about 6.6% with a 0.3 decrease compared with that in 2015. However, due to the fact that the GDP deflator will only be -0.1%, the nominal growth rate of GDP will be 6.5%, a 0.1% increase compared with that in 2015. Among them, the growth rate of the first industry will remain almost the same; the growth rate of the second industry will be 5.4%, a 0.5 decrease compared with that in 2015; the growth rate of tertiary industry will be slightly falling back to 8.0%.

2. the asset investment in 2016 will continue to fall back. It is estimated that the growth rate will be 9.6%. However, take the factor of price into account, the real growth rate will remain the same with that in 2015.

3. The consumption will remain stable in 2016. It is estimated that the growth rate will be 10.3%, a slight decrease compared with that in 2015.

4. With the spreading of world economic crisis and intensification of volatilities in emerging economies, the economic recovery in Europe and Japan is slow. China's external environment will continue to be in the gloom in 2016. However, due to the factor of cardinal number, the trade for the whole year will increase. It is estimated that the growth rate of export in 2016 will be 2.1%, the growth rate of import will be 1.1%. The trade surplus will be 3789.2 billion yuan (582.9 billion US dollar), a 51% increase compared with that in 2015.

5. With the dropping of global demand, continuation of super bulk commodity cycle and influence of various kinds of geopolitics, the pressure of imported deflation is still overhanging. In addition, considering the decrease of domestic demand, the price level will in 2016 remain at a low level. It is estimated that CPI will be 1.3%, the negative growth of PPI will be slowing down, and the deflator of GDP will be -0.1%

6. The economic downturn will make the public finance situation even worse. It is estimated that affected by continuous shrinking of fund income, the government revenue will only increase by 2.1% compared with that in 2015

2. 2015, the Year Unveiling the Crucial Stage of the New Normal State

In 2015, Chinese macro-economy entered into the crucial stage of its new normal state. Affected by both factors with a trend and factors with seasonality, various kinds of macro-economic indexes have changed beyond expectation, and various kinds of risks have gone up to a large extent; Meanwhile, the structural adjustments went to a deeper level, prosperity showed up in depression, vitality and motivation was nurtured in economic transition, and traces of local stability began to appear in economic downturn. In general, Chinese economic performance in 2015 featured the following six characteristics:

Table 2-1: Macro-economic Indicators 2015-2016

Predictors	2014	2015 (accumulation)			
		Quarter 1	Quarter 2	Quarter 3	Quarter4 (E)
1. Growth rate of GDP (%)	7.4	7.0	7.0	6.9	6.9*
Added value of the primary industry	4.1	3.2	3.5	3.8	4.0*
Added value of the secondary industry	7.3	6.4	6.1	6.0	5.9*

(Contd.)

Predictors	2014	2015 (accumulation)			
		Quarter 1	Quarter 2	Quarter 3	Quarter4 (E)
industry	8.3	6.1	6.0	6.2	5.9*
Added value of the tertiary industry	8.1	7.9	8.4	8.4	8.2*
2. Total asset investment in society (billion yuan)	50200.5	7751.1	23713.2	39453.1	55220.6*
(growth rate, %)	15.7	13.5	11.4	10.3	10.0*
Total retail sales of social consumer goods (billion yuan)	26239.4	7071.5	14157.7	21608	29020.8*
(growth rate, %)	12.0	10.6	10.4	10.5	10.6*
3 . Export (billion yuan)	14391.2	3149.3	6572.2	10236.5	14204.1*
(growth rate, %)	4.9	4.9	0.9	-1.8	-1.3*
Import (billion yuan)	12042.3	2394	4959.4	7633.4	10597.2*
(growth rate, %)	-0.6	-17.3	-15.5	-15.1	-12.0*
Trade surplus (billion yuan)	2348.9	755.3	1612.8	2603.1	3606.9*
(share of GDP, %)	3.7	5.1	5.1	5.3	5.3*
4. Growth rate of M2 (%)	12.2	11.6	11.8	13.1	13.3*
Total financing in society (billion yuan)	16460	4610	8810	11940	15192.6*
5. Growth rate of resident consumer price indicator (%)	2.0	1.2	1.3	1.4	1.4*

(Contd.)

Predictors	2014	2015 (accumulation)			
		Quarter 1	Quarter 2	Quarter 3	Quarter4 (E)
Growth rate of GDP deflator(%)	0.8	-0.3	-0.1	-0.3	-0.5*
6. National governmental income (billion yuan)	19444.3	4512.6	9694	14157.8	19024.4*
Growth rate (%)	7.2	-6.2	-3.7	-2.6	-2.2*
National general public budget income (billion yuan)	14035	3640.7	7960	11441.2	15129.7*
Growth rate (%)	8.6	3.9	6.6	7.6	7.8*
Growth rate (%)		2.4**	4.7**	5.4**	5.4**
National government-controlled income (billion yuan)	54093	8719	17340	27166	38947*
Growth rate (%)	3.5	-33.3	-33.2	-30.5	-28.0*
Growth rate (%)		-30.4**	-29.5**	-26.4**	-24.0**

2.1. Constant downturn of economic growth

In 2015, the growth rate of China's GDP decreased continuously to 6.9%, 0.4% lower than that of 2014. Chinese macro-economy stepped into a period of fast slump. If we consider various kinds of statistic criteria and structural factors of macro-economic indicators, we could see that decline of all kinds of nominal growth and individual indicators are much larger than the decrease of real growth rate of GDP. Direct feelings of various kinds of economic actors about economic deterioration were much worse than what was reflected in the real growth rate of GDP statistically.

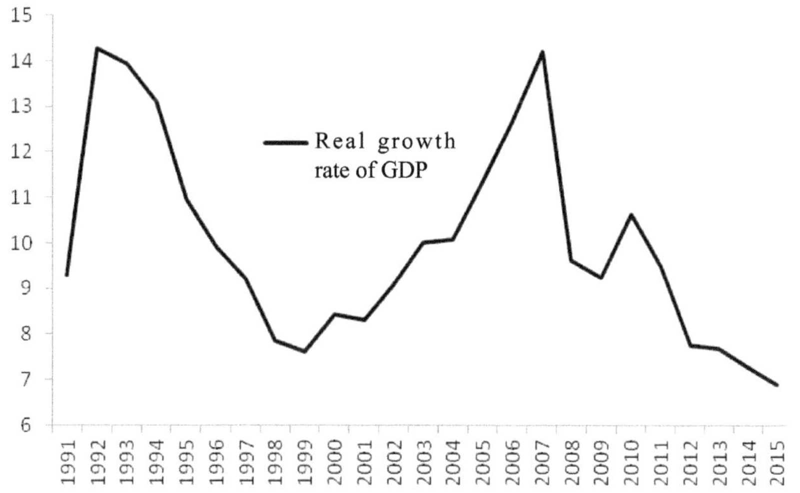

Figure 2-1 China's real growth rate of GDP over past 25 years

1). In 2015, the new low point over the last 25 years. Since 1991, China's annual GDP growth rate have never been under 7%. Comparing current situation with the gloom period of Chinese economy between 1997 and 2001, the Chinese macro-economy had began to enter a deep-level downturn stage under the effects from both factors with a trend and with seasonality. The growth rate was even 0.7% lower compared with that at the bottom point during the years from 1997 to 2001.

2). Affected by continuous spreading of deflation, nominal growth rate of GDP slowed down to a larger degree. For the fist time over the past 5 years, nominal growth rate of GDP was lower than real growth rate. In the first three quarters of 2015, the nominal growth rate of GDP was only 6.6%, a 1.8% decrease compared with that at the same period to time in 2014 and a 1.5% decrease compared with that for the whole year of 2014. According to the current estimation, the GDP deflator of the fourth quarter will further go down, which will result in a nominal GDP growth rate of 6.4%, a 1.7% decrease compared with that in 2014. This nominal GDP growth rate will reach a new low over recent years, which will appear to be quite recessionary to people.

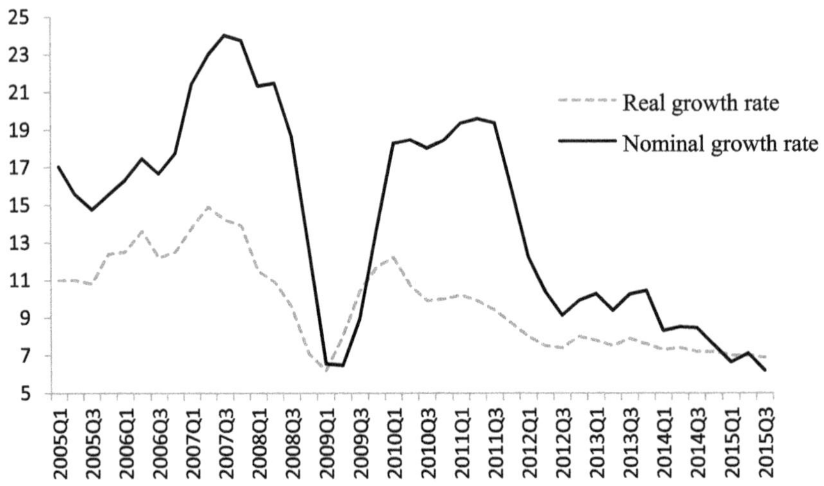

Figure 2-2 China real and nominal growth rate of GDP

3). Considering the super-high speed growth of financial sectors supported by recessionary bubbles in 2015, the extent of decrease of Chinese economic growth rate will be larger if financial sectors are not taken into account. In that case, the real growth rate of GDP is only 5.4%, a 1.2% decrease compared with that in 2014; the real growth rate of tertiary industry is only 6.9%, a 0.2% decrease compared with that in 2014.

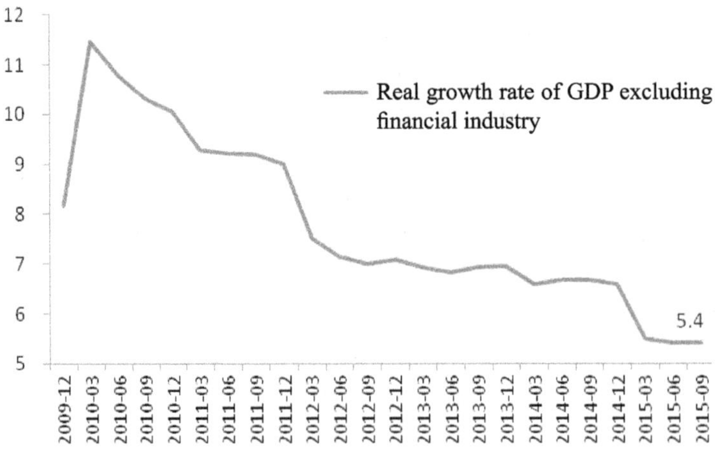

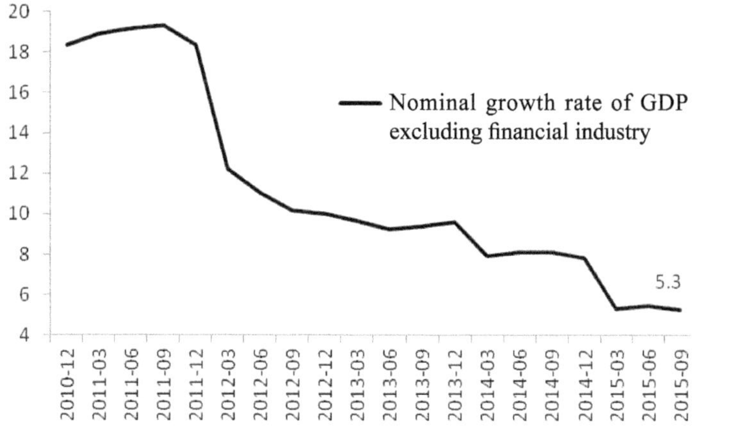

Figure 2-3 Macro-economic growth parameters excluding the financial industry

4). Judging from the regional structure, the nationwide GDP growth rate of 6.9% indicated collapses in some local economic growth, which was particularly reflected in the exponential economic decline happened in the North-east China and some other regions. In the first three quarters of 2015, the real growth rate of GDP of Liaoning, Heilongjiang, Shanxi and Hebei Province was respectively 2.7%, 5.5%, 2.8% and 6.5%, whilst the nominal growth rate was respectively 0.2%, -2.2%, -1.2% and -2.0%. The nominal growth rate of Inner Mongolia and Gansu was respectively only 0.2%, -2.2%, -1.2% and -2.0%. The huge decline of economic growth in these regions directly resulted in the deviation of all kinds of indicators and deterioration of socio-economic issues.

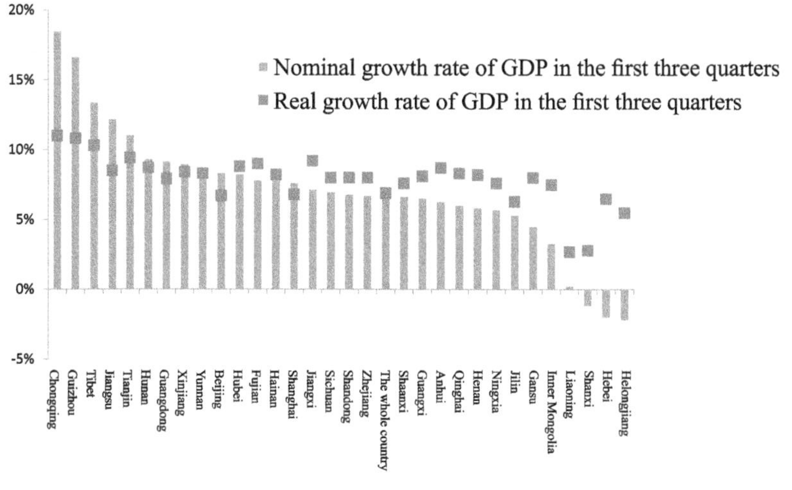

5). From the perspective of industrial structure, the GDP growth rate of 6.9% just uncovered the wide-spreading industrial depression. It is estimated that the growth rate of industrial added value is only 5.9%, a 2.4 decrease compared with that in 2014. Moreover, the nominal growth rate of industrial added value had declined to zero by the end of 2015, and the industrial main business income came across negative growth.

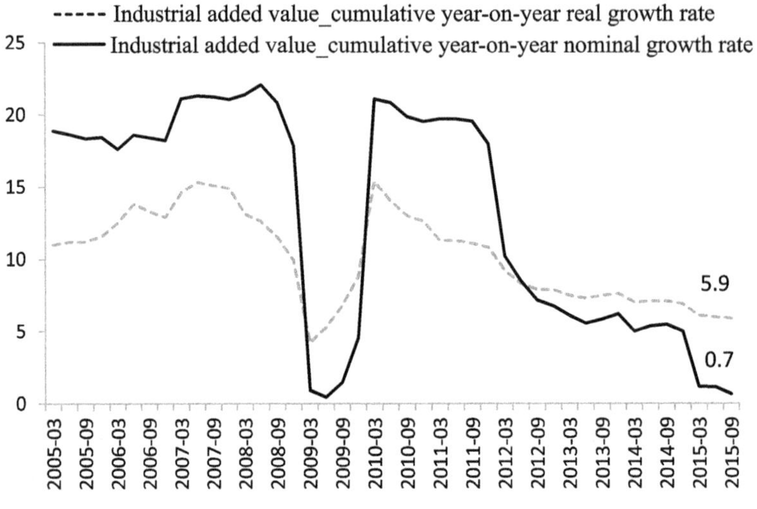

Figure 2-5 Significantly weak industry

6). From the perspective of demand structure, the GDP growth rate of 6.9% also meant that export, investment and demand fell back in an acceleratory way. The insufficiency of effective demand was looming large. The cumulative growth rate of asset investment was 10.0% in 2015, a 5.7% decrease compared with that in 2014. Particularly, the growth rate of manufacture investment was 8.3%, a 5.5% drop compared with that in 2014. The growth rate of real estate investment was 2.0%, a 10.4% decline compared with that in 2014. Decreasing investment is the core factor of the current economic downturn. The Cumulative growth rate of export in 2015 was -1.3%, a 7.4% decrease compared with that at the same time in 2014, which showed a consecutive declining situation. However, considering the fact that price of export went down, the extent of decrease in the quantity of export was relatively smaller. What was worth our attention was that another parameter that reflected domestic demand – growth rate of import – dropped down drastically in 2015. The cumulative growth rate of import in 2015 was -15.0%, a 15.4% decrease compared with that in 2014.

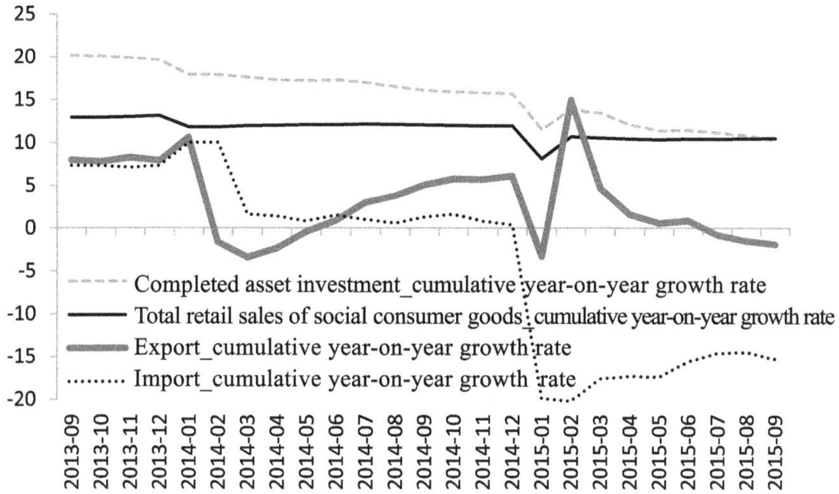

Figure 2-6 Decline in three major demands

7). With a growth rate of 6.9%, the Chinese enterprise performance indicators were deteriorating. Their profits met with "negative growth period". Among them, the profits of industrial enterprises declined substantially. Figure 2-7 showed that total profits of above-scale industry from January to September of 2015 decreased by 2.1% compared with that at the same time of 2014. The growth rate decreased by 11.9% compared with that at the same time of 2014, and decreased by 15.5% compared with that at the same time of 2013. Among them, stark changes were seen in the state-owned enterprises. The profits of the state-owned enterprises from January to September of 2015 decreased by 24.7%, and the growth rated decreased by 30.1 % and 32.7% respectively compared with those at the same time of 2014 and 2013.

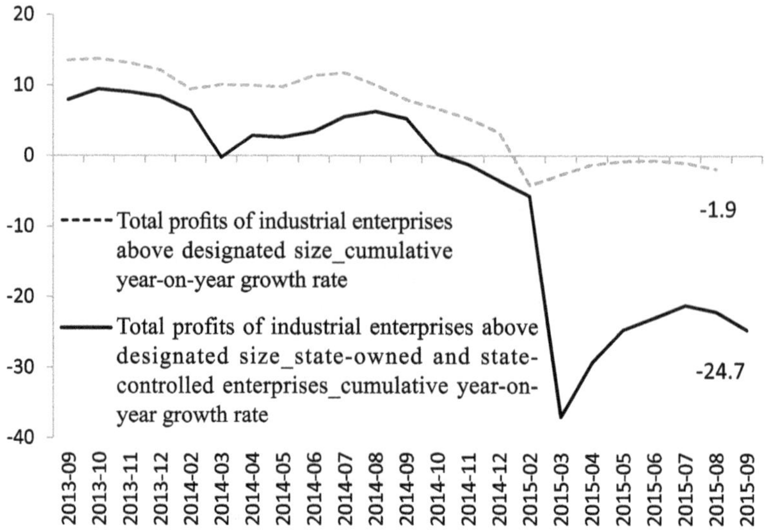

Figure 2-7 Rapid decline of industrial enterprise profits

Meanwhile, the deficit scale of industrial enterprises had the tendency to expand. The number of loss-making enterprises increased by 13.6% year-on-year, with the growth rate increased respectively by 10.5% and 11.6% compared with 2014 and 2013 on a year-on-year basis. Comparatively speaking, the total deficit of the enterprises running under deficit rose to a larger extent, with a 22.8% rise from January to August. The growth rate of deficit increased by 12.9% and 31% respectively compared with 2014 and 2013 on a year-on-year basis. The change of state-owned enterprises was the largest. The total deficit from January to September increased by 34.7%, a 24.5% and 51.7% increase compare with that in 2014 and 2013.

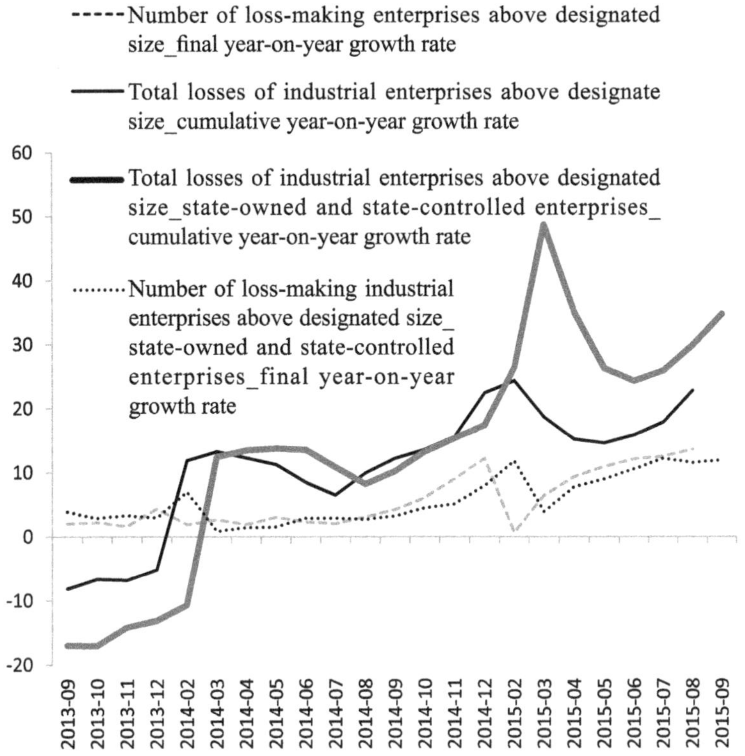

Figure 2-8 Area of loss-making was expanding

At the same time in which industrial profits growth was negative, there was noticeable decline in the growth rate of bank profits. The growth rate was only 1% from January to September, 8% higher than 2014 on a year-on-year basis. It is estimated that the growth of bank profits will be negative at the fourth quarter of 2015.

8). The government revenue began to decrease. Some regions and areas witnessed stark change, causing difficulties to the public finance operation of local governments. From January to October of 2015, national public financial revenue increased cumulatively by 7.7% (5.4% with same statistical criteria), respectively a 2.7% and 3.2% lower than the year of 2014 and 2013. There were sharp decrease in some provinces and municipalities. For instance, the growth rate of government revenue in Liaoning and Heilongjiang provinces respectively decreased by -27.4% and -15.8% year-on-year from January to September, 20% lower than that of 2014 on a year-on-year basis. As another example, the growth rate of government revenue in Shanxi from January to September was -11.4% year-on-year, 16.8% lower than the same period of 2014. Such a rapid decrease was totally beyond expectation toward 2014, and it made many local governments tumble into the predicament regarding income and expenditure.

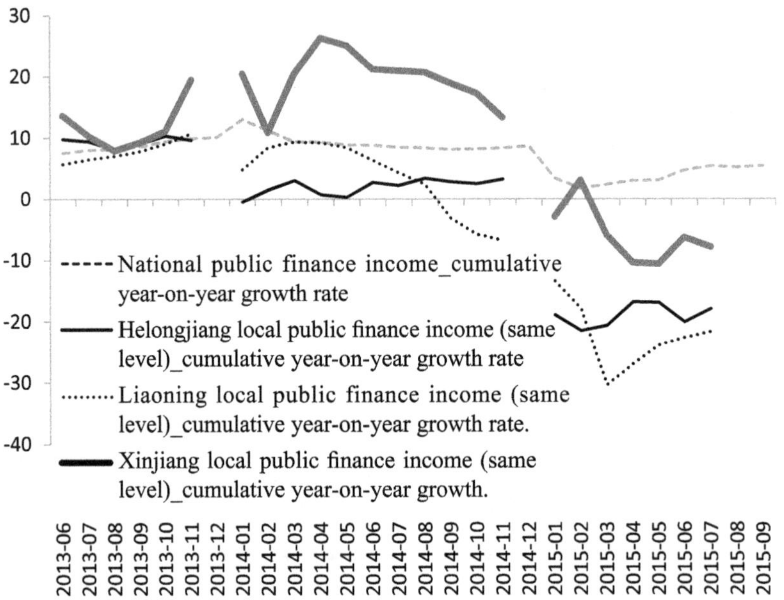

Figure 2-9 Significant public finance downward

Meanwhile, another source of revenue for local governments – land transfer fees decreased in a large degree during the adjustment of real estate industry. From January to September, the area of land bought by real estate developers increased by -33.8% year-on-year, a 29.2% decrease comparing to the same period of 2014. However, the purchase price of land increased -27.5% on a year-on-year basis, a 39.0% increase comparing to the same period of 2014. This resulted in a decrease of 30.5% in revenue from funds controlled by governments, or a decrease of 26.4% with the same statistical criteria.

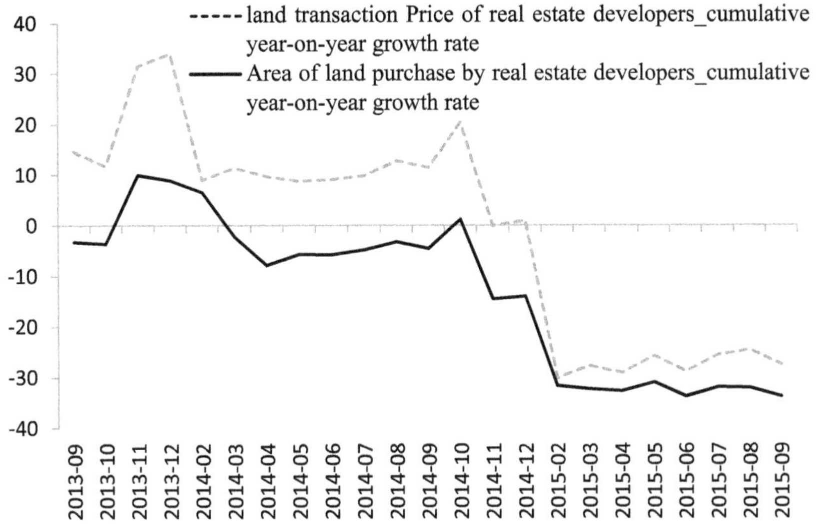

Figure 2-10 Sharp decrease of land development

According to the current estimation, the general public finance of 2015 will reach 15.1 trillion yuan, a 7.8% increase on a year-on-year basis, or a 5.4% in crease with the same statistical criteria; revenue from funds will be 3.9 trillion yuan, a -28% increase on a year – on –year basis; total government revenue will reach 19 trillion yuan, a -2.2% increase year-on-year. 2015 will be the year in which the Chinese government revenue steps into a difficult period.

Table 2-2: Change and composition of governmental income

Predictors	**2014**	**2015 (cumulation)**			
		Quarter 1	**Quarter 2**	**Quarter 3**	**Quarter 4 (E)**
National governmental income (billion yuan)	19444.3	4512.6	9694	14157.8	19024.4*
Growth rate (%)	7.2	-6.2	-3.7	-2.6	-2.2*
National general public budget income (billion yuan)	14035	3640.7	7960	11441.2	15129.7*
Growth rate (%)	8.6	3.9	6.6	7.6	7.8*

(Contd.)

Predictors	2014	2015 (cumulation)			
		Quarter 1	Quarter 2	Quarter 3	Quarter 4 (E)
Growth rate (%)		2.4**	4.7**	5.4**	5.4**
National government-controlled fund income (billion yuan)	5409.3	871.9	1734	2716.6	3894.7*
Growth rate (%)	3.5	-33.3	-33.2	-30.5	-28.0*
Growth rate (%)		-30.4**	-29.5**	-26.4**	-24.0**

Figures marked with * are estimated.

Figures marked with ** are growth with same statistical criteria excluding the impacts of some government-controlled funds turned general public budgets.

9). Although the household income maintained stable relatively, from mid-term perspective all kinds of income will decline with the drop of GDP growth rate. In the first three quarters of 2015, the national household per capita disposable income was 16367 yuan with a nominal growth of 9.2% year-on-year , or a real growth rate of 7.7% without taking the factor of price into account. Among them, the urban household per capita disposable income was 23512 yuan with a nominal growth of 8.4%, or a real growth rate of 6.8% without taking the factor of price into account; the rural household per capita disposable income was 8297 yuan with a nominal growth rate of 9.5%, or a real growth rate of 8.1% without taking the factor of price into account. Comparing with the highest growth during recent time, the growth rates declined respectively by 6.5% and 3.6%. what was worth attention was because of the difference among parameter basis on which the factor of price was left out, there had been inconsistency between the growth rates of GDP and nominal income level, i.e. , the nominal growth rate of GDP was around 6% while the growth rate of nominal household income was around 9%-10%. This reflected that there was excessive distribution in national household income distribution with the growth rate of salary higher than nominal growth rate of DGP. However, from mid-term perspective, this phenomenon will not maintain.

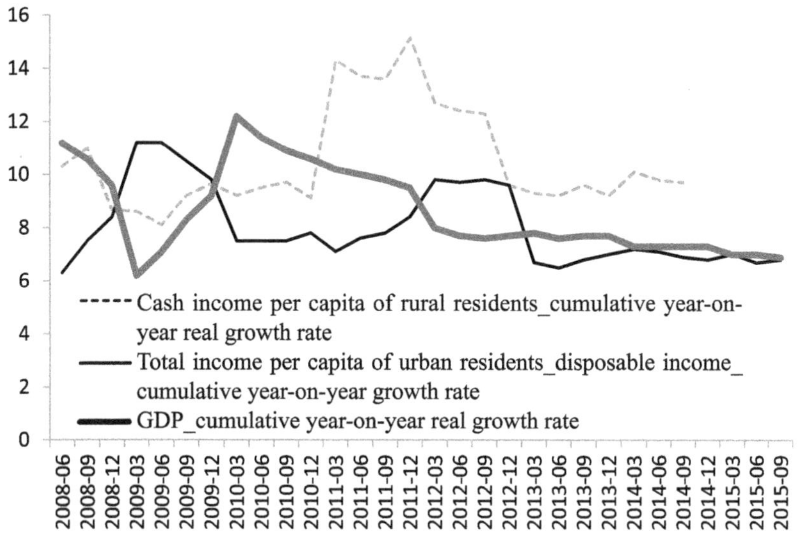

Figure 2-11 Residents income went down with GDP downturn

10). With the growth rate being 6.9%, the labour market is changing in a abnormal way. The potential risks of structural unemployment and comprehensive employment are forming and gradually clearer.

Due to the fast development of service industry and the encouragement on masses for entrepreneurship and innovation, at the time being the general situation of labour market remains stable judging from major official indicators. The newly employed population of urban areas in 2014 had reached 1360 0000, and the number was 1066 0000 in the first three quarters of 2015. The official recorded and surveyed unemployment rate was generally about 4.1% and 5.22%. Therefore, it seems that the situation of labour market goes well in a general way.

However, with the constant decline of economic growth, the factor of employment support has been fading away. Some potential risks existing in the labour market has already began to be clear.

First, the high-frequency data showed that the labour market is weakening. Since last year, the employment rate indicator of PMI from manufacture and service industry has been dropping down below 50 one by one, which is the threshold diving prosperity from recession. This proves that employment has been shrinking.

Second, although the requirement rate indicator of labour market was larger than 1, since the middle of 2013, the population needed by labour market and seeking for employment has been decreasing, which indicated that the labour market has been shrinking. In the first quarter of 2015, the population needed by labour market and seeking for employment substantially declined by 16.6% and 17.0% respectively corresponding to the same time in 2014; the population needed by labour market and seeking for employment in the second quarter declined by 5.4% and 2.7% respectively, which are larger than the decrease in 2014 in general.

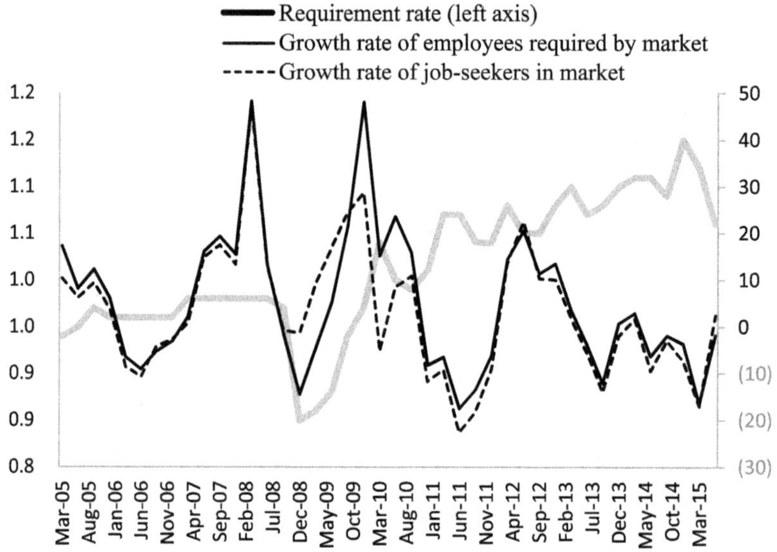

Figure 2-12 Mixed situation of labor service market

Third, the second industry continuously went down in an acceleratory way. Since 2003, the urban employment growth has mainly came from the rapid expansion of service industry, while the employment of second industry has been decreasing in a consecutive three year. In both 2013 and 2014, the employment growth rates in second and tertiary industries were all 0.3% with a annual average population decrease of 70 0000. Comparing to the annual population growth of 760 0000 seen from 2003 to 2012, this turning-point change was worth our concern. In 2015, the second industry will be absolutely exclusive to labour force in a consecutive third year, which will be a population of 354 0000. This will be more exclusive comparing to the past two years. Among them, the construction industry expanded very slowly with a population growth of only 119 0000; industrial sectors will continue to release labour force with a population decrease of 473 0000

Fourth, the expansion momentum of tertiary industry began to show signs of weakening, particularly the consumption-oriented service industry which holds the largest share in employment witness the most substantial decrease in expansion momentum. Although the tertiary industry is still absorbing a large number of labour force with a employment population growth of 1727 0000 comparing to 2015, the growth rate is nearly the same. Among them, the employed population in the real estate industry increased 55 0000; the employed population in the manufacture-orientied service industry has a increase of 5450000, and the growth rate is slightly increased; the consumption-oriented service industry has a increase of 911 0000, and the growth rate is largely going down, which is the major factor causing the reduction of expansion momentum in the tertiary industry.

Fifth, the growth of urban employment was slowing down. The net growth of urban population decreased from 1370 0000 in 2010 to 1070 0000 in 2014. In the first three quarters of 2015, the newly employed population was 1066 0000, a 1.5% decrease comparing to 2014. Another phenomenon reflecting the increasing employment pressure is the slow-down of salary increase.

Sixth, the migration of farmer-turned workers slowed down drastically. From 2010-2012, the annual growth of total population of farmer-turned workers was 1094 0000. In 2013, the number decreased to 6330000. In 2014, the number went down further to 5010000. According to the current data, by the end of the second quarter of 2015, the total population of farmer-turned workers was 17436, a 0.1% increase year-on-year, which meant the migration of farmer-turned workers almost stopped. This indicated that the labour market has been affected by the economic downward, which was mainly evident in the drastic slow-down of migration of farmer-turned workers. For the next step, an increase in unemployment rate will be seen.

Seventh, the operational difficulty leveled up with the constant economic downturn in those industries with overcapacity as well as some traditional manufacturing industries, which were at the brink of bankruptcy. The problem of labour market is turning from inadequate newly employed population to rising unemployment rate. With some enterprises undergoing restructuring and bankruptcy, the problem of lay-off in heavy-industrial enterprises and state-owned enterprises began to show up. For instance, many steel and coal enterprises has already stopped production with a serious hidden unemployment.

Eighth, the labour market of China has some structural problems, such as difficulties in the employment of university graduates. The number of university graduates has rapidly increased from 114 0000 in 2001 to 749 0000 in 2015, which takes up 70% of the goal for urban newly employed population. The employment pressure is ever going up. If the problem of university graduates could not be solved properly, it would not only cause depreciation and waste on human resource, but also trigger a series of social problems. Besides, challenged by new business models such as "internet +", entrepreneurship, which has produce a large number of self-employment oriented jobs, but at the same time has also destroyed plenty of traditional professions, is undergoing the throes of creative destruction.

2.2. Overall Emergence of Deflation

Affected by factors such as inadequate overall demand, endogenous austerity and declining price of international bulk commodities, the problem of deflation in the field of industry went down to a deeper level with the consumption price index dropped to between 1% and 2% and the GDP deflator being overall negative. The pressure of deflation is increasing.

1. The price parameters has been dropping down constantly, which indicated that this round of deflation was getting worse day by day and was in rapid expansion. This was manifested in the following aspects:

First, the price of import and export has been persistently tepid with the price of import index being negative for 42 months. Meanwhile, the price of export index has fluctuated around 0 for 40 months. In August of 2015, the growth rate of export price index was -3.5%, which decreased by 5.6% comparing to the same time of 2014; the growth rate of import price index was -15%. It has been negative for consecutive 40 months, and reached a new level during recent period, which was 14% larger than the rate of decrease at the same time in 2014. This indicated that the problem of imported deflation not only didn't get alleviated, but also was compounded.

Second, the factory gate prices of industrial products index and purchase price index has been negative for a consecutive 43 months, and the year-on-year decline rate has been increasing. In September of 2015, the factory gate prices of industrial products index was only -5.9%, a 4.1% decrease in growth rate compared to the same period of 2014; the purchase prices of industrial products index was only -6.8%, a 5.9% decrease in growth rate compared to the same period of 2014. This indicated that the overall deflation in the industrial field has been further compounded.

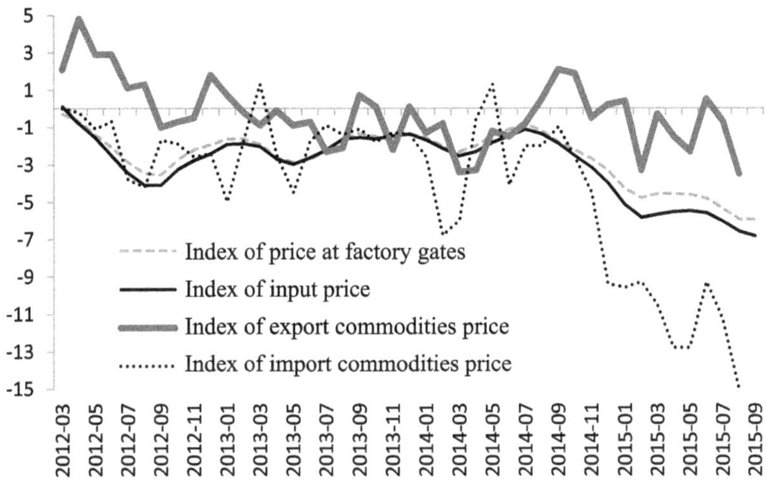

Figure 2-13 Various price indexes in continuous decline

Third, the CPI continued to fall back to the extent which was far below the target prices, and started to stay between 1% and 2%. In October of 2015, the growth rate of CPI was 1.3% , a 0.3% decrease comparing to the same period of 2014. Among them, the food CPI year-on-year growth was 1.9%, or only 0.9% without taking food into account, which was a 0.3 % decrease comparing to the same period of 2014. The core CPI excluding food and energy year-on-year growth rate was 1.5%, a 0.1% rise comparing to the same period of 2014. Although the CPI year-on-year growth was not trapped in deflation, there was something worth attention: (1) The constant dropping of CPI has already changed the way of operation in which the GDP growth rate decreased while the CPI growth rate was stable from 2011 to 2013. This indicated that the inadequate demand was more important as one of the major factors contributing to the decrease of GDP growth rate. (2) the CPI at all levels has been lower than 2% for 15 months, and far below the target of 3% set up by government.

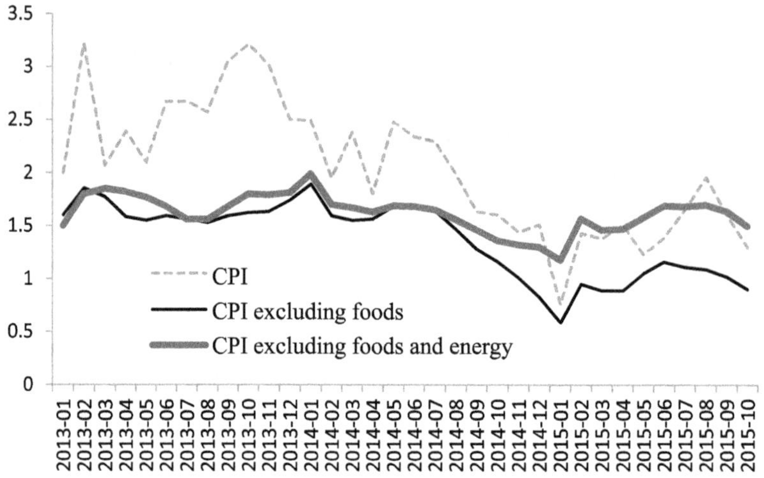

Figure 2-14 Significant CPI decrease at all levels

Fourth, the GDP deflator, which was closer with macro-economy situation, has always been negative. This indicated that the Chinese macro-economy might began to enter into "depression era" in an all-round way. In the first three quarters of 2015, the GDP deflator was -0.3%. Among them, the GDP deflators in the first and third quarters was all negative, being -0.3% and -0.7% respectively. This indicated that the total price level corresponding to social final goods and services was already in the state of deflation. This state only appeared twice in the past 25 years: the first appearance was from the second quarter of 1998 to the fourth quarter of 1999 with the average level being -1.25%; the second appearance was from the first quarter to the fourth quarter of 2009 with the average level being -1.4%. Those two periods are all the times when the Chinese economy came across overall depression. This demonstrates that if the Chinese economy goes along the way we saw from the first to the third quarter of 2015, it will be very likely to tumble into overall depression once again.

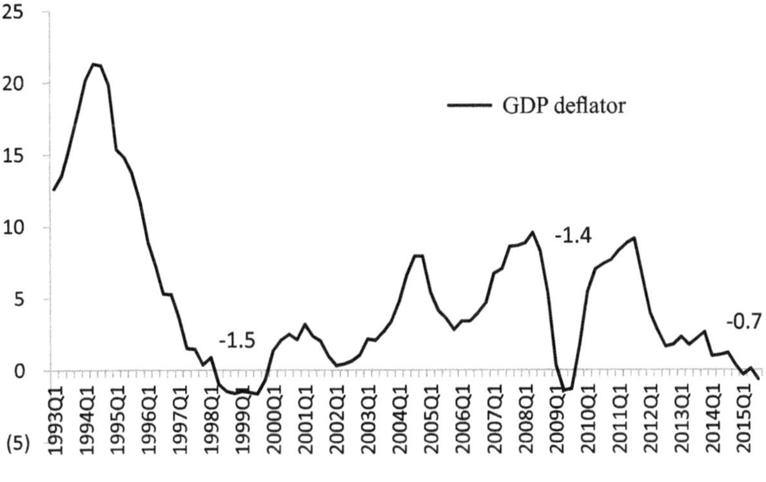

Figure 2-15 The third lowest point of GDP deflator over the past 20 years.

2). Compared with historical development, this round of deflation was the most severe one in the past 25 years. First, the cycle of deflation was the longest. Among the five-year deflation between 1007 and 2002, there was a period of recovery from 1999 to 2001. This was an equivalent of two cycles of price. There was only 1 year of deflation between 2008-2009, which was a stress response to the sudden attack from global financial crisis. The current deflation has been over three years and a half since the beginning of 2012. However, it does not bottomed yet without any signs of recovery. Therefore, it is estimated that the cycle of this deflation will at least cost 6 years.

Second, the current deflation is similar to the previous ones. It has the longest time in which PPI decreased more than 4%, and its largest decrease was 5.9%, the same as that between August and October of 2015, which was also higher than 5.7% which we saw in the November of 1998.

Third, in the current deflation, the gap between CPI and PPI continues to be widening. Its time of staying in the positive interval surpassed all periods of deflation in history. General speaking, when economy is in the state of deflation, the decline of PPI will be larger than that of CPI; while the economy is in the state of recovery, the rise of PPI will also be larger than that of CPI. This is the internal mechanism of economic cyclical adjustment. In the current deflation, the gap between CPI and PPI has already be in the positive interval for 4 years with the highest point being 7.9% in August of 2015, which was much higher than 4.5% in November of 1998 and 6.7% in August of 2009.

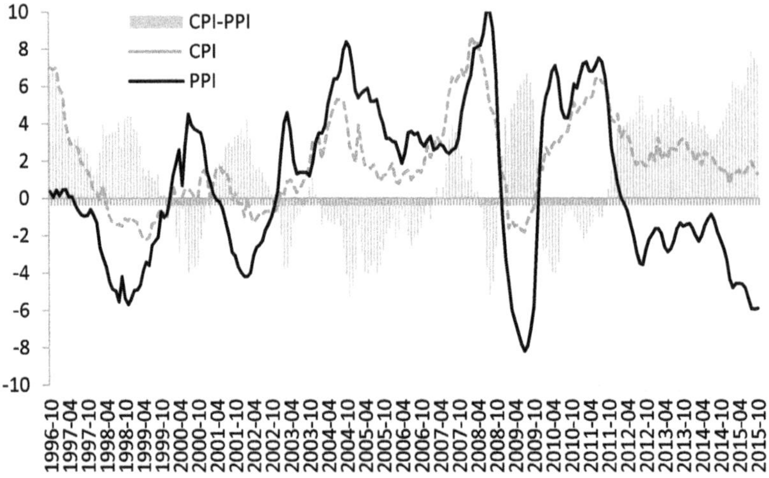

Figure 2-16 This round of deflation was the most severe one over the past 20 years

Fourth, the most serious moments of the current deflation were all in the third and fourth quarter of 2014, which means the end of the current deflation is still far. For the time being, it might be the worst situation, but might also not be the bottom.

3). Comparing with other countries in the world, China's price level is not only way below the average level of developing countries, but also becomes closer and closer to the price level of those countries which implement quantitative-easing policy. According to the forecast made by IMF, the worldwide average CPI will be 3.3% with the CPI of developed countries being 0.31% and emerging economies being 5.6%. Hence, the price level of 1.3% in China by the end of 2015 will be nearing that of developed countries, and significantly lower than developing countries.

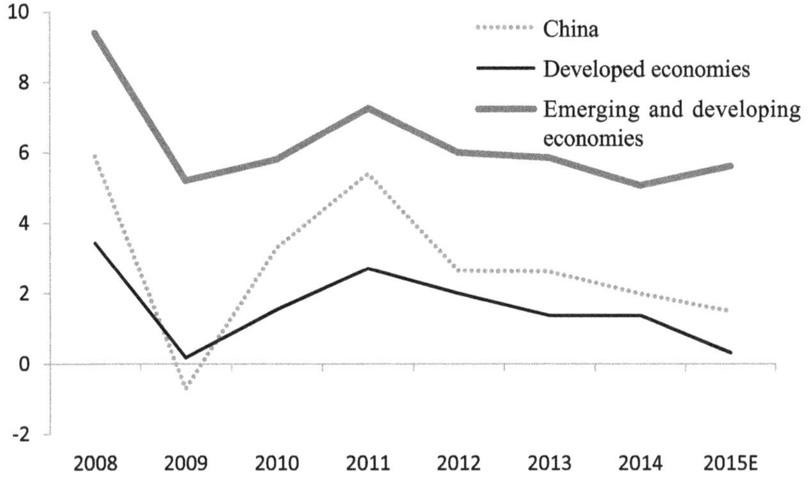

Figure 2-17 International Comparison of CPI

2.3. Persistent downturn of business climate index

At the same time when all kinds of consistent indexes are slipping down, the macro-economy business climate indexes are continue to fall back, staying at a low level. This demonstrated that the inertia and trend of Chinese economic downturn in 2015 has already taken shape.①

1). Li Keqiang index dropped significantly, reaching a new low over that past 5 years.

Li Keqiang index was 6.5%, a 2.0% decrease comparing with 2014, breaking the second lowest record since its advent, which was only higher than a index of 6.2% in February of 2009. The power generation, freight traffic and credit amount, which are components of Li Keqiang index, have showed synchronized downturn. Particularly, the cumulative growth rate of power generation and freight traffic was the lowest comparing with the past years since 2009. The cumulative growth rate of national freight traffic was 4.1%, and the national power generation was only 0.1%

① In this book, the calculation formula of Li Keqiang Index is as the follow: Li Keqiang Index= growth rate of power generation×40%+ growth rate of loan balance×35%+ growth rate of freight traffic×25%。

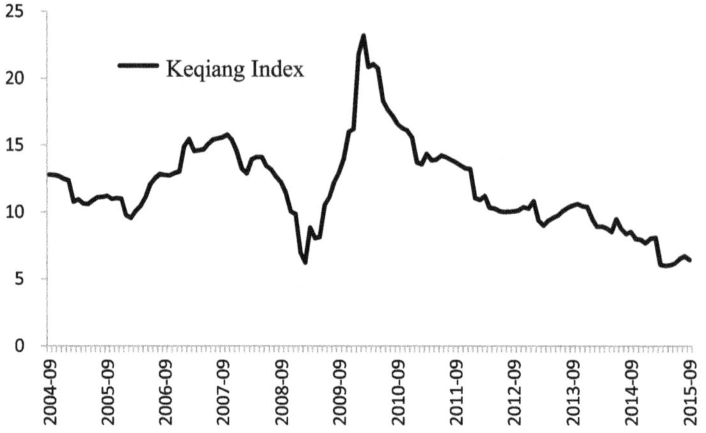

Figure 2-18 Declining Keqiang Index

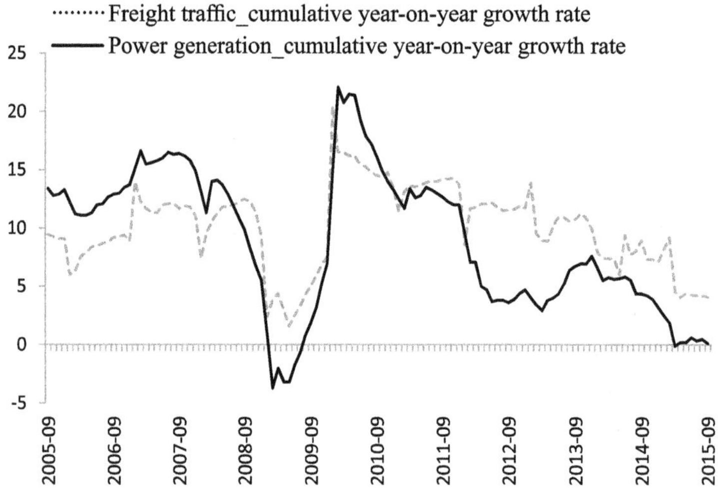

Figure 2-19 Decreasing power generation and freight traffic

2). The downturn of the investment and trade leading parameters all demonstrated the further spreading of market softness. This is mainly reflected in the following aspects: first, the investment leading parameters, i.e., the total investment of planned construction projects and newly launched construction projects this year were all growing with a low pace. The cumulative growth rates from January to October were respectively 5.3% and 4.1%, a 6.2% and a 9.3% decrease comparing with the same period of 2014, reaching a new low over the past 5 years as well as the third lowest point after 1998 and 2008 over the past 25 years. Second, PMI of manufacture industry remained below the mid-point of 50. In October of 2015, PMI was 49.8% according to the date released by the National Statistical Bureau. This indicated that the entire market of manufacturing industry was still weak. Third, BDI has been constantly declining since 2013, and showed signs of heading for bottom in the fourth quarter of 2015. By now, BDI is only 721, which is relatively low from historical perspective.

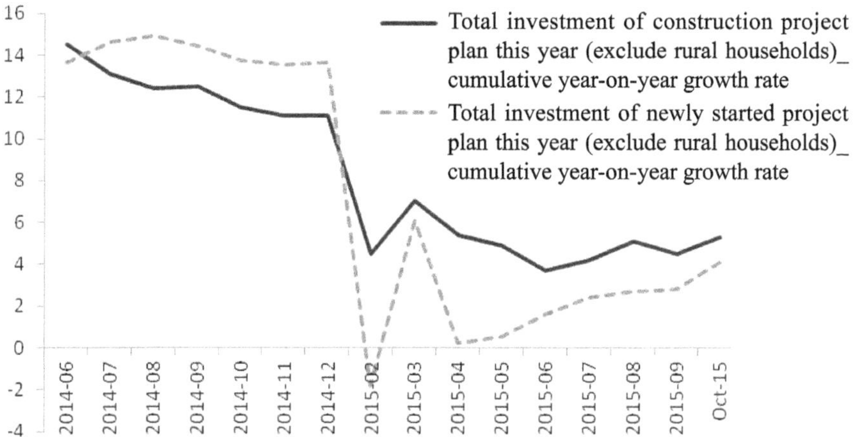

Figure 2-20 Leading data of investment in slump

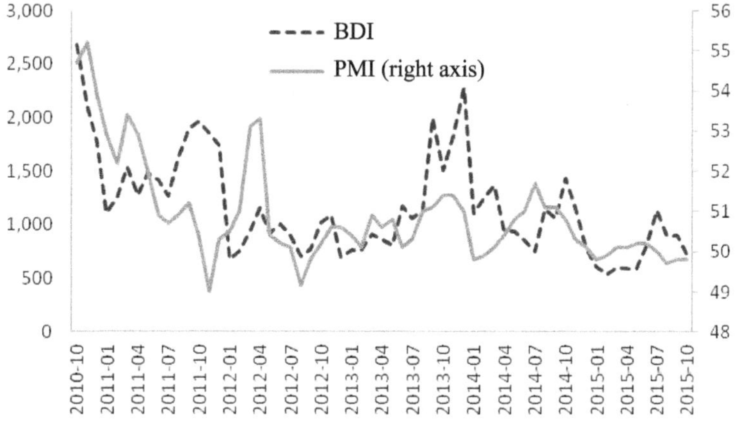

Figure 2-21 BDI and PMI were at historical low

3). All kinds of confidence indexes also continued to slip back. Low confidence and expectation are core reflection of economic endogenous contraction. This was mainly illustrated in the industrial enterprises confidence index. In the third quarter of 2015, the index was 50.5, a 13.1% decrease compared with the same period of 2014; the economist confidence index was 3.55, a 0.87% decrease year-on-year; the banker confidence index was 40.6, a 18.5 drop year-on-year; the consumer confidence index remained relatively stable from 2014 to 2015, but a slight decline was also noticed in the third quarter compared with the second quarter.

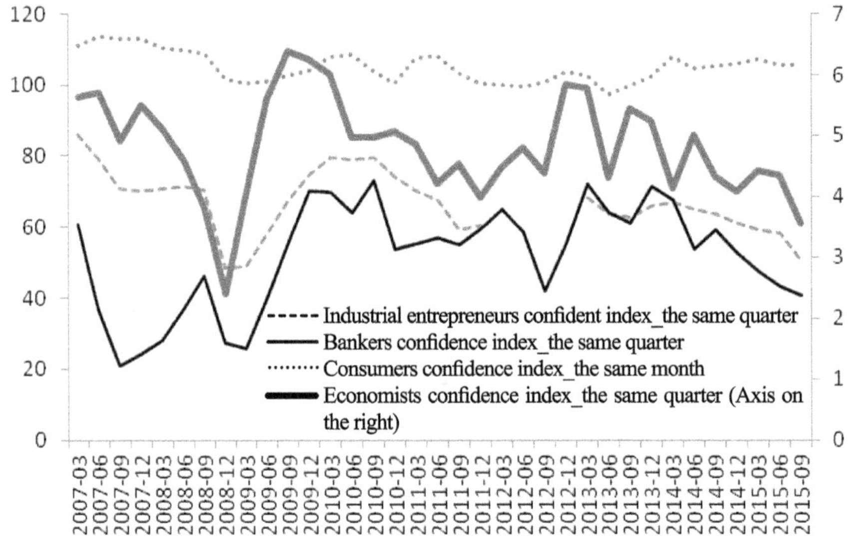

Figure 2-22 Various kinds of confidence indexes were on the decrease

4). The constant downward of the macro-leading composite index, coincident composite index and lagging composite index reached a new low over the recent years. In August of 2015, the macro-coincident composite index was 92.94, which was lower than the lowest point of 93.84 in February of 2009. The change of these parameters all showed clearly that the inertia and internal force pulling down the Chinese macro-economic growth have already taken shape, which could lead to further deterioration of current depression.

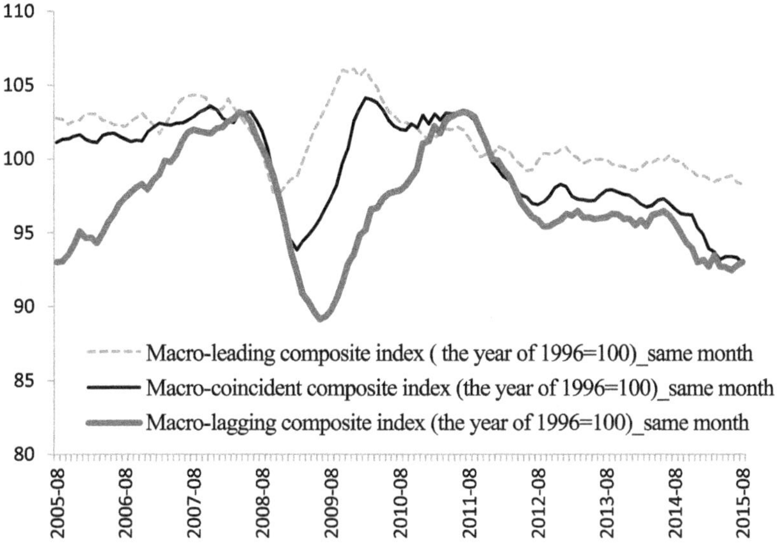

Figure 2-23 Constant downturn of macro-leading, coincident and lagging composite indexes

2.4. Deep differentiation of the economic structure

Against the backdrop of overall weakness of macro-economy, the deep differentiation happened within Chinese economic structure. As a result, we saw prosperity existing in overall depression and vitality as well as new driving force hidden inside the transformation. The structural adjustment has been further deepened.

1). Regional differentiation happened in the national overall economic slow-down with co-existence of prosperity of those provinces which succeeded in economic transition and depression of those provinces which was stuck in economic transition.

In the process of economic downturn nationwide, some provinces and municipalities still kept good momentum of growth, for example, in the first three quarters of 2015, the nominal growth rate of GDP of Tianjin, Jiangsu, Chongqing, Guizhou and Tibet were still on double-digit level. Particularly, the nominal growth rate of GDP of Chongqing and Guizhou were respectively 18.4% and 16.6%. The growth rate of government revenue of Tianjin, Jiangsu, Chongqing and Jiangxi also reached two figures, respectively 11.6%, 10.4%, 12.0% and 13.6%. The high GDP growth rate laid a foundation for smooth operation in these regions.

However, at the same time, the north-east China and some other provinces and municipalities experienced stark qualitative change. For instance, in the first three quarters of 2015, the real growth rate of GDP in Liaoning Province was 2.7%, the nominal growth of GDP was 0.2%; the real growth rate of GDP of Heilongjiang Province was 5.5%, but the real GDP growth was -2.2%; the GDP real grow rates of Hebei and Shanxi Provinces were respectively 6.5% and 2.8%, but the nominal growth rate were -2.0% and -1.2%. This has led to substantial decline of government revenue in these regions. For example, in the first three quarters of 2015, the year-on-year growth rates of government revenue of Shanxi and Jilin Province were respectively -11.4% and -3.7%. Heilongjiang and Liaoning experienced more drastic drop in government revenue with year-on-year growth rates being -15.8 and -27.4%. This directly resulted in malfunction of these local governments.

Table 2-3: Severe Regional Differentiation

Provinces and municipalities	Regions with substantial declining growth rate					Regions with relatively steady growth rate				
	Ji lin	Shan xi	Liao ning	He bei	Heilong jiang	Tian jin	Jiang su	Jian gxi	Chong qing	Gui zhou
Real growth rate of GDP	6.3	2.8	2.7	6.5	5.5	9.4	8.5	9.2	11.0	10.8
Nominal growth rate of GDP	5.3	-1.2	0.2	-2.0	-2.2	11.0	12.2	7.1	18.4	16.6
The growth rate of government revenue	-3.7	-11.4	-27.4	6.5	-15.8	11.6	10.4	13.6	12.0	5.6

2). Driven by various factors such as demand and policy, the change of engine for economic growth also led to dramatic differentiation in all kinds of industries. While the traditional industries continued to drop down, the strategic emerging industries showed strong momentum of growth.

First, affected by demand transition and policy support, the strategic emerging industries rose up against adversities. For example, according to the statistics from the China Association of Automobile Manufacturers, from January to September of 2015, 17,091,600 automobiles were produced and 17,056,500 were sold, with the output decreased by 0.82% year-on-year and the sales increased by 0.31% year-on-year. Particularly, 2,48 5,3 00 commercial vehicles were produced and 2.508,700 were sold, with the output decreased by 12.48% year-on-year and the sales decreased by 11.83%. However, at the same time, 144284 new energy automobiles were produced and 136733 were sold, with the output increased by 2.0 times year-on-year and the sales increased by 2.3 times. Particularly, 93032 pure electric automobiles were produced and 87531 were sold, a year-on-year increase respectively by 2.0 times and 2.7 times. Take another example, from January to September of 2015, the total amount of telecommunication service was 1656.23 billion yuan, a 25.3% increase on a year-on-year basis, which rose up by 10.3% comparing to the same period of 2014 and 0.7% higher than the growth rate from January to August. The total amount of telecommunication service demonstrated an acceleratory rise.

Second, differentiation was seen between traditional manufacturing industry and new manufacturing industry. From January to September of 2015, electronic information manufacturing industry maintained a high growth rate, with the the cumulated growth rate of above scale electronic information manufacturing being still as high as 10.7%. Although this was 1.2% lower than the same period in 2014, it was still 4.5% higher than the average level of industry (6.2%). In the first three quarters of 2015, the completed software business income from the software and information technology services was 3112.7 billion yuan, an increase of 16. 5% on a year-on-year basis; the completed total profit was 344.6 billion yuan, an increase of 9.4% on a year-on-year basis. Although the growth rates were still 4.1% and 12.3% lower respectively than the same period in 2014, they were still higher than that of the average level of the industry. In contrast, the conventional and special equipment manufacturing industry was plummeting, with the growth rate being 3.4% from January to September of 2015, 4.5% lower than the same period in 2014. It was also 3.6% lower than than the aggregate growth in the manufacturing sector.

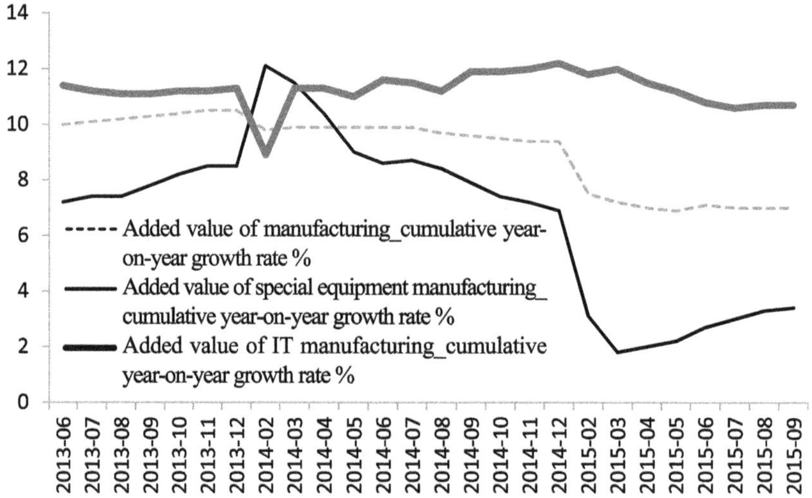

Figure 2-24 Differentiation within manufacturing

Third, the growth rate of new consumption and new consumption industry was still rapid, but some of the traditional consumption showed a relatively large decline. From January to September of 2015, the retail sales growth rate of the consumer goods above designated size was only 7.5% with a decline to a certain extent. What was pulling the industry down was car sales, with a grow rate of only 4.2% from January to September of 2015, 5.0% lower than that in 2014. However, the growth rate of communications equipment reached 35.8%, 11.5% higher than that in 2014.

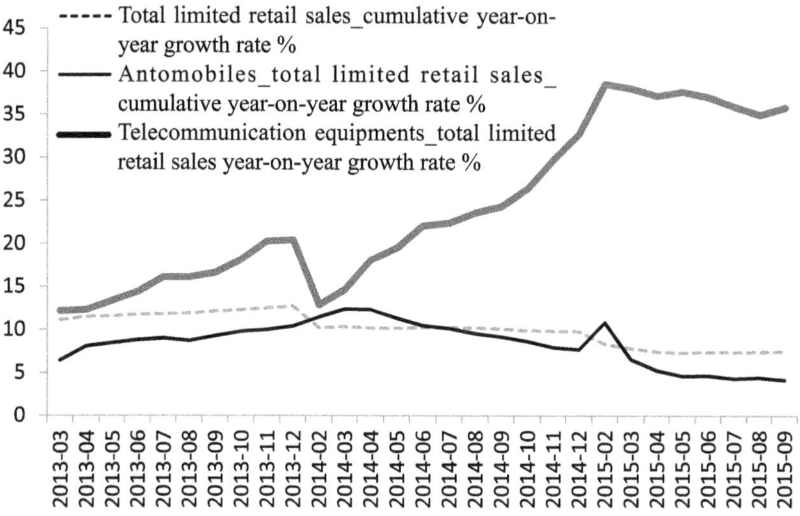

Figure 2-25 Significant consumption differentiation

Fourth, differentiation in industry profits was more serious in the overall decline. This was mainly reflected in the fact that the net profit of banking industry, chemicals industry, non-ferrous metal industries, machinery, equipment industry, retail industry and other listed companies in the first half of this year showed basically zero growth. Meanwhile, the steel industry and the coal industry was declining persistently. The growth rate of net profit in Iron and steel industry in the first half of this year was s -288.8%, while the downturn of net profit in the coal industry was more than 68.6%. At the same time, the representative of the new economic growth pole of the biopharmaceutical industry showed high growth in a relatively stable way. Over the past three years, the growth rate will remained at around 20%. With the pick-up of real estate sales showing signs of recovery, the growth rate of profit in real estate industry appeared to be a strong rebound in the first half of 2015, rising from -21.5% in the third quarter of 2014 up to 38,8% in the second quarter of 2015.

Growth rate of net profits of banking

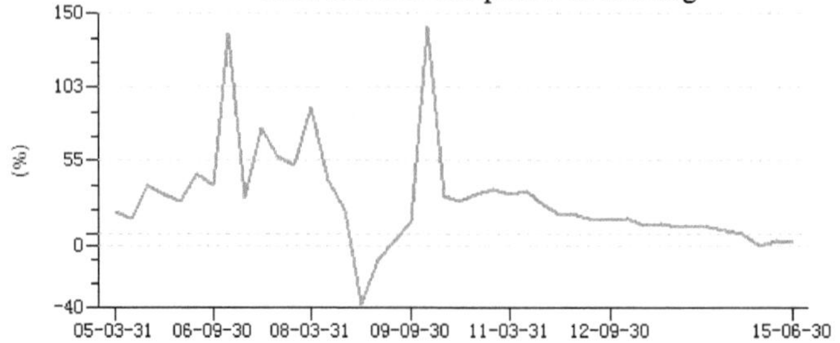

Growth rate of net profits of banking (%)

Source: Wind information

Growth rate of net profits of cheminal raw materials industry

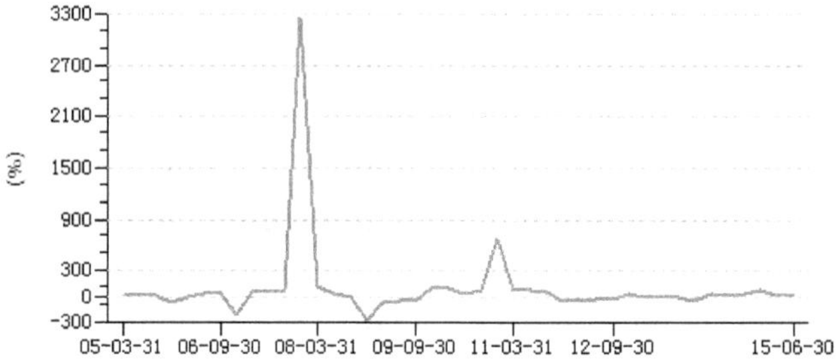

Growth rate of net profits of cheminal raw materials industry (%)

Source: Wind information

Growth rate of net profits of mechanic equipment industry

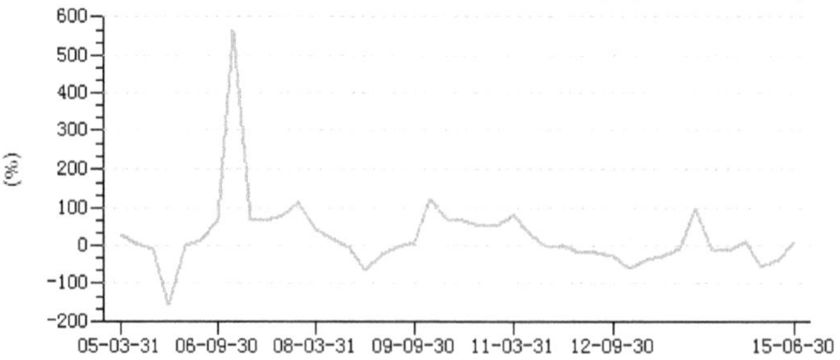

Growth rate of net profits of mechanic equipment industry (%)

Source: Wind information

Growth rate of net profits of non-ferrous metal industry

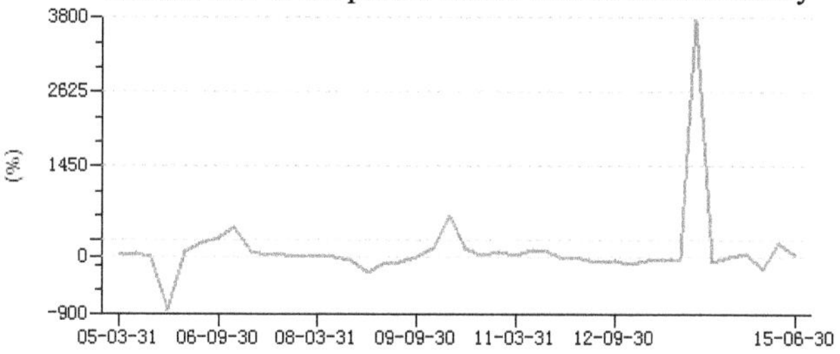

Growth rate of net profits of non-ferrous metal industry (%)

Source: Wind information

Growth rate of net profits of steel industry

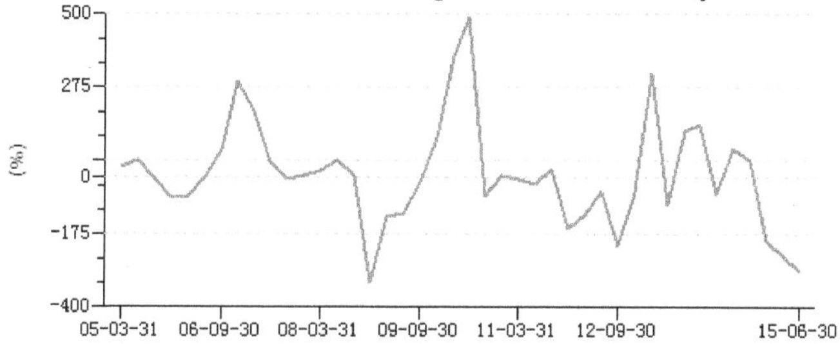

Growth rate of net profits of steel industry (%)

Source: Wind information

Growth rate of net profits of coal industry

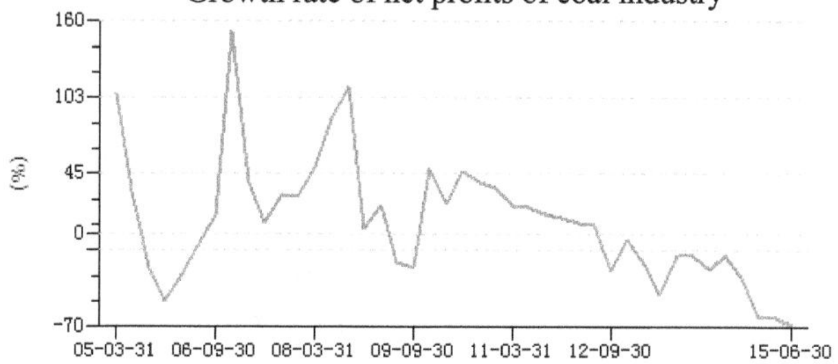

Growth rate of net profits of coal industry (%)

Source: Wind information

Growth rate of net profits of pharmaceutical industry

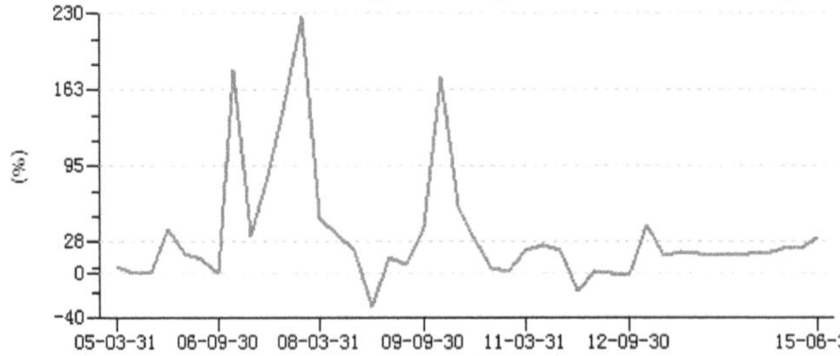

Growth rate of net profits of pharmaceutical industry (%)

Source: Wind information

Growth rate of net profits of real estate industry

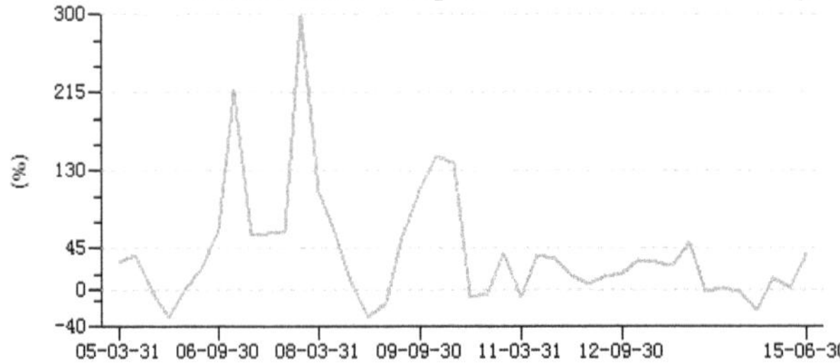

Growth rate of net profits of real estate industry (%)

Source: Wind information

Figure 2-26 Net profits growth rate of different sectors among listed enterprises

3). With the intensification of economic differentiation, especially the long-term depression which has trapped the provinces stuck in economic transition and traditional manufacturing industry, the market forces for the Chinese economic structure adjustment have already taken shape, thus the economic structure adjustment is further expedited and deepened.

Judging from the current situation in which the traditional industry is declining while emerging industry is rising up with new growth poles, the structural adjustment of China begins to enter into the most difficult phase. A new landscape is badly called for. This is mainly reflected in the intensification of relative price adjustment in 201j5. Several major relative prices has been undergoing constant adjustments since 2008, which formed a strong structure adjustment force oriented by market that went into a stable state by the end of 2011. Among them, the price index of heavy and light industries maintained at around 0.98 since the end of 2011, and the price index of services and industrial products maintained at around 1.00 since the end of 2011. China's terms of trade, though experienced fluctuation in a few months, maintained at around 1.02 since the end of 2011. Until the end of 2014, three years has been passed since the market oriented relative price adjustment and the according industrial structure adjustment started in China. Therefore, theoretically the rising of emerging leading industries and their replacing the old industries are around the corner. However, since the end of 2014, the relative price and heavy and light industries, as well as the relative price of export products and import products has undergone a new round of intensive adjustment. The relative price of heavy and light industries quickly dropped from 0.98 in September of 2014 to 0.93 in September of 2015, and the size of decline was as large as 5%. The relative price of import and export products quick rose from 1.03 in September of 2014 to 1.14 in September of 2015, and the size of increase was as large as 11%. This indicated that the Chinese economy has been undergoing world structural adjustment which has been further deepened.

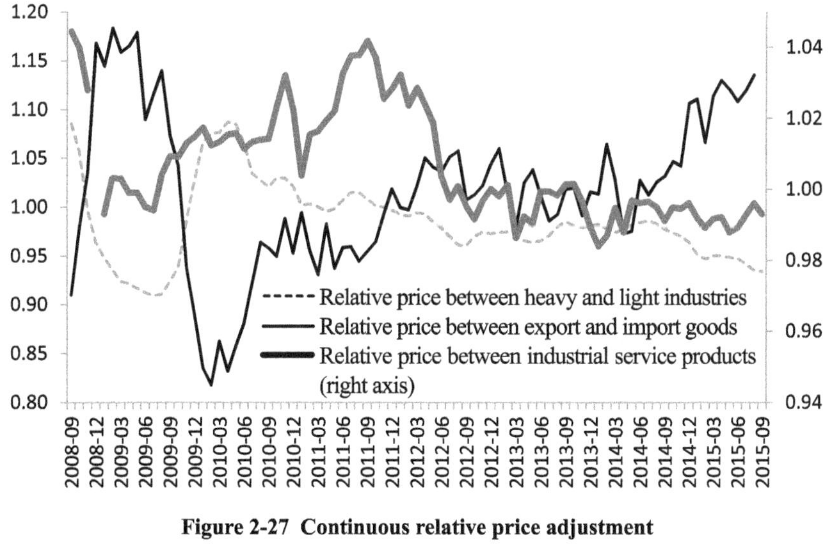

Figure 2-27 Continuous relative price adjustment

2.5. The bust of stock market bubble

In the state of overall market downturn, in 2015 the Chinese stock market experienced rapid forming of bubbles, sudden blast of bubbles and the subsequent painful absorption of bubbles. All of these posed huge and constant impact onto the macro-economy.

1). the accelerated generation of stock market bubbles caused deviation between production profits and financial profits, which resulted in the co-existence of depression in production sectors and bubbles of financial market. From the second half of 2014 to the firs half of 2015, at the same time when the real estate industry was undergoing constant adjustments, the stock market was roaring. As a result of this, the stock market bubbles replaced the real estate bubbles. In the first two quarters of 2015, the real estate market basically maintained the setup in 2014 during differentiation . The national housing climate index dropped from 97.21 in the end of 2013 to 92.4 in May of 2015. From January to May of 2015, the investment growth rate of real estate development was 5.1%, 9.6 % lower than the same period in 2014. The area of land purchased for real estate development decreased by 31% year-on-year, 25.3% lower than the same period in 2014. The area of land for the newly launched real estate construction increased by 5.3 year-on-year, 6.7% lower than the growth rate of the same period in 2014. The price-income ratio of national commercial housing was near 7, which was a decline compared with 7.1 in 2014 and 7.3 in 2013. The real estate bubble has been curbed at that stage.

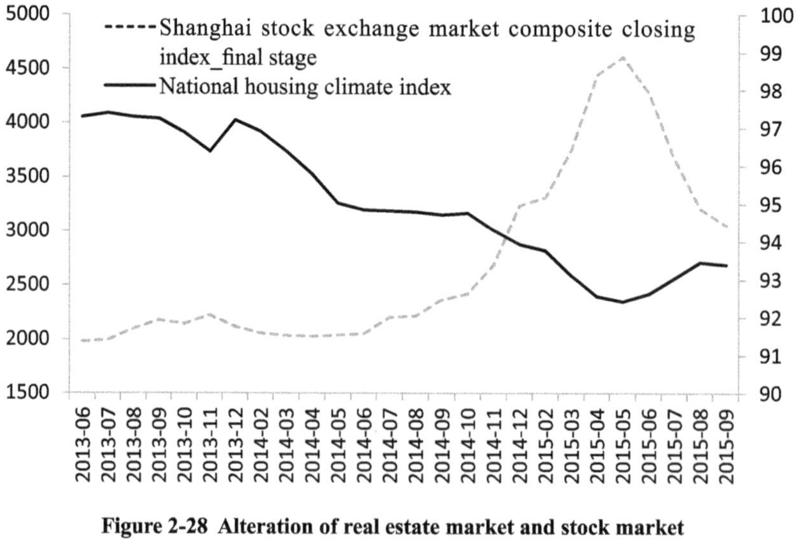

Figure 2-28 Alteration of real estate market and stock market

However, affected by various factors such as policy adjustment, system reform, structural elements and liquidity shift, starting from June of 2014 and developing within less than one year, the Shanghai Stock Exchange Index increased from 2010 to 5178 in June of 2015, the Shenzhen Stock Market Composition Index rose from 7134 to 18198, the small and medium sized board index increased from 4556 to 12084, the growth enterprise market index increased from 1303 to 4088. This quick rising

Directly led to an acceleratory pick-up of price-earning ratio of the stock market. From the end of 2014 to the end of 2015, the price-earning ratio of A share in Shanghai stock market index rose from 14.20 times to 21.66 times; the A share of Shenzhen stock market index rose from 35.94 times to 73.62 times,; small and medium-sized board index rose from 42.59 times to 86.97 times; the growth enterprise market index increased from 63.76 times to 144.12 times. China's A share turnover also increase by 8 times.

When the stock market bubble was booming, the deviation between production profits and financial profits was further enlarged, which led to the con-existence of depression in production and bubbles in financial market. Although this kind of deviation between financial growth and industrial growth was not something new, but its overall qualitative change happened during the period from the fourth quarter of 2014 to the first half of 2015. This was mainly reflected in the following aspects: first, driven by the quick recovery of stock market, the growth rate of added value in financial sector quick rose from 9,7% in 2014 to 17.5% in the first half of 2015, while the growth rate of added value in industry declined from 6.9% in 2014 to 6.0% in the first half of 2015. Second, the growth rate of stock market value increased from -3.2% to 161.7% year-on-year, while the growth rate of total profits of industrial enterprises declined from 9.8% in May of 2014 to -0.8% in May of 2015.

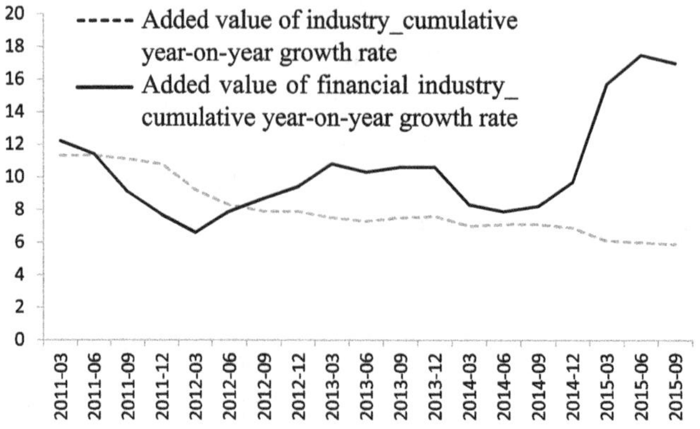

Figure 2-29 Separation between financial growth and real economy development

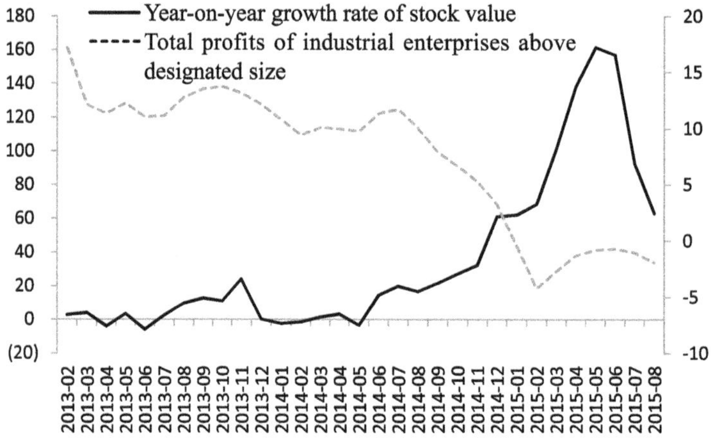

Figure 2-30 Separation between financial returns and real economy benefits

2). The sudden blast of stock market bubble had a great impact on the real economy. At the same time when the leverages such as margin were used to boost the stock market, giant bubbles were also produced: first, with over-rapid rising of all kinds of parameters, the market was teeming with speculation. For example, the new stock market accounts in the first quarter increased by 433% year-on-year, with a highest record of 440 new accounts opened up in one week. Among the account holders, 62% of them were young people born between 1980 and 1990. More than 300 stocks limited on average per day. Second, the leverage is excessive for stock market investment. The balance of margin reached 2.240 billion in June, which accounted for 20% of the stock market inflows. Meanwhile, the ratio of unlisted financing could be as high as 1:5. Using leverages to boost stock market will make it very fragile as a whole, because the financing leverage and forced selling will lead to a consequence that the decrease rate of the stock market will be much faster than its increase rate. Third, the high price-earning ratio meant there was obvious bubbles, especially in the A share of Shenzhen stock market, the small and medium-sized board and growth enterprises board. For example, the price-earning ratio of A share in Shenzhen stock market reached 73.62 in the end of May, which was the second highest point since 2000. The annual yield which correspond to this price-earning ratio was about 1.4%, far below the level of risk free market returns. The TTM reached 86.97, making a new high record. The annual yield corresponding to this price-earning ratio was 0.7%. Fourth, the net profit growth of listed enterprises was unable to support the rising of stock price. The net profit growth is the core factor determining the medium and long-term stock price of enterprises. In 2015, the listed enterprises as an entirety will have negative growth with the profits rate of many industries falling below zero. The overall rise of stock price will incur mid-cause adjustments.

In June of 2015, the stock market bubble suddenly blasted. In less than one month, Shanghai stock market index fell from the highest point of 5178 to 3507 of July 8 with the decline being 47.6%. Subsequently, the stock market fell into recession. Although the government persistently made policies to support the stock market, the stock market index constantly declined in fluctuations. The total market value decreased from 6275 billion yuan in June to 4380 billion yuan in August with the decline being more than 30%.

Table 2-4: P/E ration of Chinese stock market

Dates	A share of Shanghai stock exchange market (TTM)	A share of Shenzhen stock exchange market(TTM)	CSI 300 (TTM)	Small and medium sector (TTM)	Growth Enterprise Market (TTM)
2015-05-27	21.66	73.62	18.01	86.97	144.12

(Contd.)

Dates	A share of Shanghai stock exchange market (TTM)	A share of Shenzhen stock exchange market(TTM)	CSI 300 (TTM)	Small and medium sector (TTM)	Growth Enterprise Market (TTM)
2014-12-31	14.20	35.94	12.91	42.59	63.76
2013-12-31	9.69	29.26	8.92	35.94	60.30
2012-12-31	11.75	26.97	11.00	28.33	34.35
2011-12-30	11.06	23.06	10.45	26.81	36.07
2010-12-31	16.73	39.67	15.34	48.99	70.75
2009-12-31	30.75	76.45	28.49	55.31	79.09
2008-12-31	13.93	17.57	12.93	21.91	
2007-12-28	47.64	58.32	43.41	68.59	
2006-12-29	36.67	51.67	32.32	39.95	
2005-12-30	18.19	34.92	14.28	21.69	
2004-12-31	21.48	27.16		31.36	
2003-12-31	36.68	48.67			
2002-12-31	44.59	183.58			
2001-12-31	40.32	55.41			

3). With the blast of stock market bubbles, that plan that using large-scale maneuver to de-leverage at macro-economic level, and the prosperity of stock market to hedge the recession in production sector failed. The huge impact at macro-economic level brought by the fast decline of stock market in a short period was far larger than those in the past. The aftermath of this bubble blast also brought about continuous negative influence to the macro-economy.

First, the equity financing plan failed, which led to the failure of strategy that aimed to reduce China's debt and leverage rate by turning debt into equity. In 2014, the cumulative financing in A share market was about 760 billion yuan, which was 2 times larger than that in 2013. Among them, IPO was about 60 billion yuan, and the re-issuing new shares and rights offering financing was about 700 billion yuan. From January to May of 2015, IPO was as large as 824 billion yuan, and the directional financing was 342.5 billion yuan, which meant that from January to May of 2015 the stock market financing reached 424.9 billion yuan. which accounted for 56% of the stock market financing for the whole year. This play a critical role in removing the financial leverage of enterprises. According to the statistics done at the beginning of June, there were more than 500 listed enterprises releasing directional re-issuance plans with the amount of financing being more than 1.500 billion yuan which surpassed the situation in 2014 in which 1320 billion yuan financing plan was released by 709 enterprises. However, with the sudden decline of stock market, some of these directional re-issuance plans failed. Compounded by the suspension of IPO, the stock financing involved was very likely to lose about 500 billion yuan. This will lead to a 4% decrease in total social financing, which will make the current recession in which liquidity is less able to permeate the real economy and financial sector meets difficulties in supporting the real economy even worse.

Second, the shattered wealth effect might lead to an obvious decline in the growth rate of consumption in the fourth quarter of 2015 as well as in 2016. Research done by Goldman Sachs indicated that the majority of calculations made on the samples base on the U.S. showed that the marginal growth of consumption propensity caused by stock market wealth in the time of one year was about 3%. Let us suppose that if China's marginal growth were 1%, it would have meant that in one year the consumption will be growing by 140 billion yuan. This will contribute 0.6 % to the growth rate of household consumption and 0.2% to GDP growth rate.

Third, the structural adjustment might be severely struck, especially for the strategy encouraging mass innovation and entrepreneurship. The reason is that large part of financing in stock market went into small and medium-sized enterprises and growth enterprise through small and medium sized board and growth enterprises board. Thus, the collapse of stocks will naturally start from the growth enterprise board as well as the small and medium-sized board. It will not only turn the investment expansion by many enterprises into unfinished projects, but will also impost too much debt on the emerging innovation-oriented talents and bust the confidence for mass innovation and entrepreneurship.

2.6. Ineffective macro-economic control policy

The macro-economic control policy was ineffective. Guided by the notion of "micro-adjustment and pre-adjustment", the micro-adjustment had never reached the goal set by the pre-adjustment. Local risks were spreading and escalating despite of the goal of "risk control". Macro-economy declined beyond expectation against the control to "maintain growth", and constantly touched the bottom; The vicious circle of "deflation-debt" became more and more explicit.

1. In the process of leverage removing, debt reduction and risk control, China followed a moderately tight monetary policy. However, the economy became ever more leveraged.

In the process of leverage removing, debt reduction and risk control, a very direct but erroneous idea was followed: a moderately tight monetary policy, which cut back on the loan raised by enterprises and debt financing of economic actors, was necessary to remove leverage, reduce debt. On the other hand, an expansionary monetary policy will necessarily lead to a large-scale rise of bank loans and other debt financing. Otherwise, debt reduction could not be realized. However, if the overall absolute reduction of leverage and debt was regarded as the short-term goal of monetary and other financial policies, the result was usually counterproductive. The excessive tight monetary policy couldn't manage the bubbles, on the contrary it would pop the bubbles and let the real economy collapse, which will give a rise to the debt ratio and trigger systematic economic crisis. Because of this, although the growth rate of M2 in China decreased from 19% in 2010 to 12% in 2014, which was much lower than the average growth rate of M2 since 1988, China's leverage ratio continued to rise instead of declining.

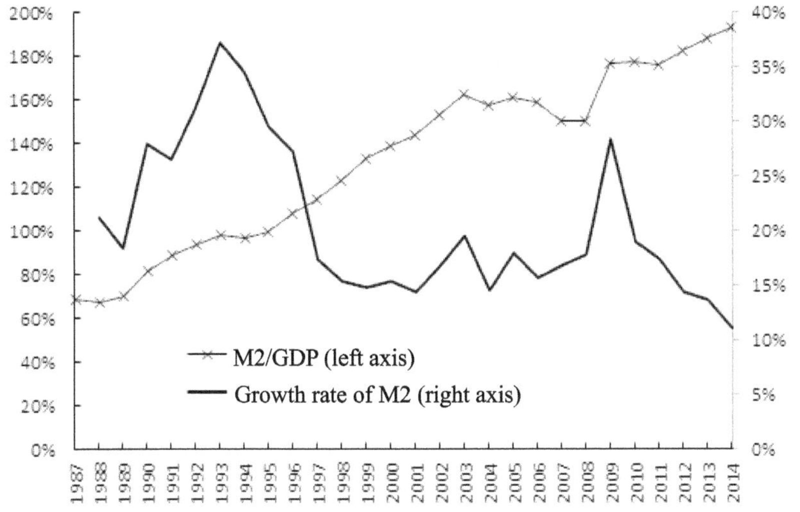

Figure 2-31 History of China's M2 growth rate（1987-2014）

If we look into the international experiences of removing leverages, we can also discover that the simple and direct logic behind current monetary policy could not be more wrong. First, the tight monetary policy carried out by Europe resulted in fast shrink of economy in countries such as Greece, in which the decline rate of economy was much quicker than that of debt, and the decline rate of debt was slower than that of asset deterioration. As such, instead of the leverage and debt ratio being reduced, economic and political crisis were sparked. Second, at the beginning of 1990's, Japan's experience also illustrated that tight monetary policy might undermine the capabilities of enterprise to pay off the debt, which would lead to the failure of leverage reduction measures. Third, the successful removing of leverages in the U.S. caused by the extremely loose monetary policy carried out by the U.S. government was proof that loose monetary policy was not in conflict with leverage removing and debt reduction.

2). Affected by off-balance-sheet clearance, bank loan cutting and overall leverage reduction, the scale of social financing was reduced and the growth rate of money supply decreased. The financial endogenous contraction was obvious. This contraction did not recovered until in 2015 the loose monetary policy was further promoted.

Affected by factors such as economic climate decline, bank loan cutting , shadow bank clearance and leverage removement, the growth rate of social financing began to decline. The cumulative year-on-year growth rate of total social financing was -7.7%, which was the same as that in the same period of 2014, and 26.9% lower than that of the same period in 2013. However, compared with the negative cumulative growth of 20.4% from January to April of 2015, this growth rate was still 12.7% higher.

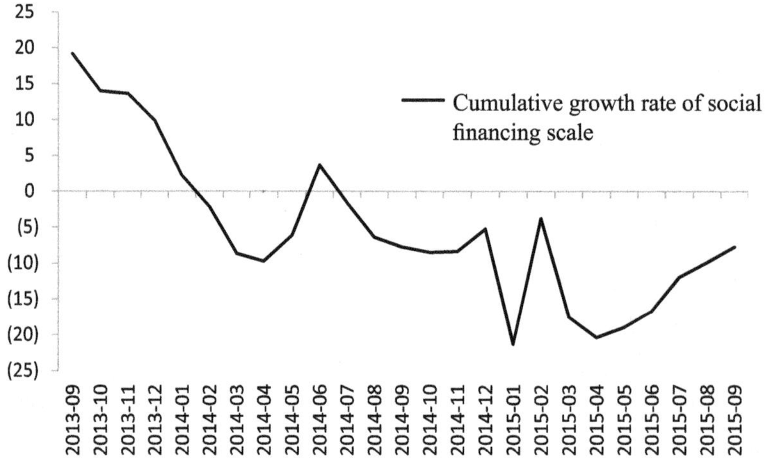

Figure 2-32 Decrease of total social financing

There were three direct causes for the decrease of social financing: first, affected by the difference between the cost of Renminbi and foreign currency financing, from January to September of 2015, the foreign currency loan was -265.91 billion yuan, a 641.51 billion yuan and 170.8% decrease compared with the same period in 2014; second, affected by off-balance-sheet business and shadow bank clearance, there were substantial decline in the entrusted loan, trust loan and bill financing, decreased respectively by 778.88 billion yuan, 303.72 billion yuan and 706.11 billion yuan compared to the period from January to September of 2014 (43.6%, 84.3% and 592.3% decline). Third, affected by the factors such as performance worsening of enterprise performance and clearance of city investment bond, enterprise bond market financing decreased by 61.13 billion yuan, a 3.3% decrease.

However, with the development of stock market and further promotion of easing-oriented policies, such trend of shrinking began to slow down in the middle of 2015. First, the total stock financing increased from 3033.36 billion yuan from January to September of 2014 to 538.22 billion yuan from January to September of 2015, which was a 77.4% increase. Meanwhile, with the further promotion of easy monetary policy, the speed of money supply began to recover to a certain degree. The growth rate of M1 from January to September of 2015 was 13.1%, 3% higher than 10.1% from January to April, and 0.2% higher than 2014 year on year. The Renminbi loans rose from 7683.18 billion yuan of January-September of 2014 to 8992.29 billion yuan of January to September of 2015, which was a 17% increase.

It is noteworthy that the phenomenon of financial endogenous contracting is still prevalence, indicated by the decline of various parameters in the circulation between credit and capital markets. First, the ever-increasing speed of monetary circulation experienced significant plummet, with a cumulative drop of 14% in 2015 compared with 2010. Second, the industrial enterprise capital turnover rate was going down, which was 2.4% from January to August, 0.05% lower than the same period of 2014 and 0.06% lower than the same period of 2013. Third, accounts receivable of enterprises and growth rate of inventory continuously decreased with the accounts receivable being 7.9% from January to August of 2015, respectively 3.4% and 4.4% lower than the same period of 2014 and 2013. The growth rate of capital used for inventory was only 2.1%, respectively 7.2% and 5.4% lower than the same period of 2014 and 2013

First, investment in infrastructure and public services was further increased in order to keep the growth rate of infrastructure investment at a high level. Despite the fact that all kinds of government revenue was decreasing, the support for investment in the second half of this year had an obvious recover. From January to September, the year-on-year growth rate of the budgetary funds in the infrastructure investment was 20.5%, 10.2% higher than that in the period between January to May, and 6.4% higher than the same period in 2014.

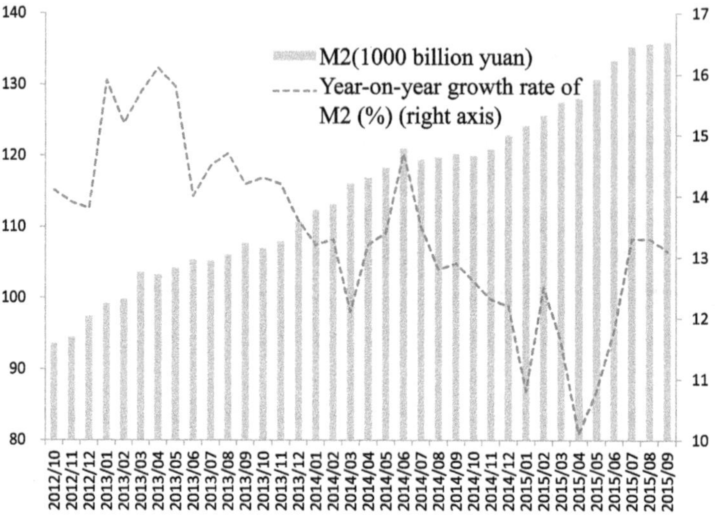

Figure 2-33 Overall decline of M2 growth rate

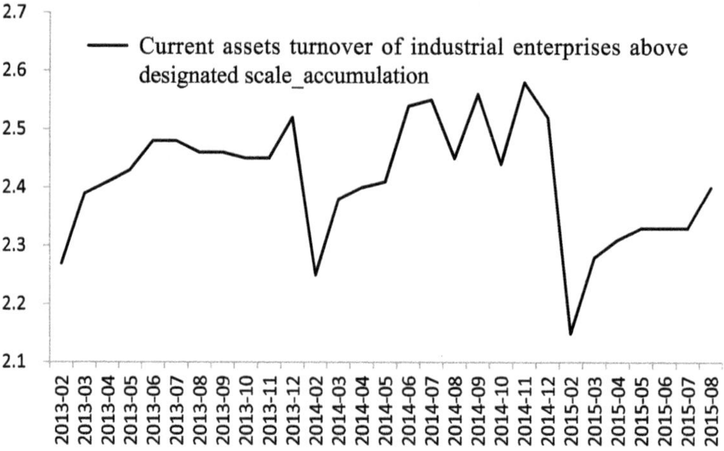

Figure 2-34 Funds turnover of real economy was slowing down

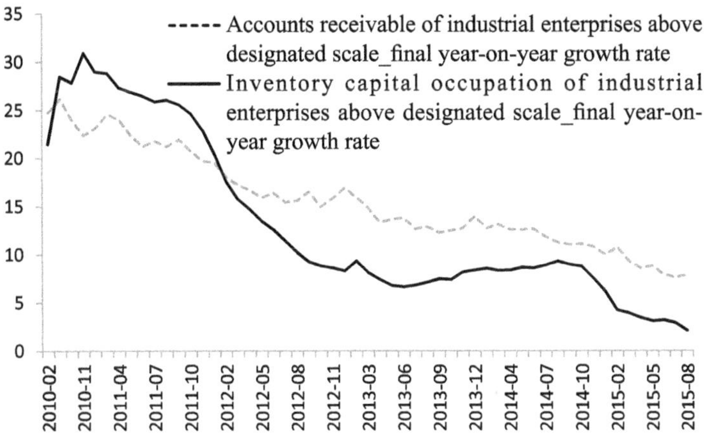

Figure 2-35 Constant decline of accounts receivable and inventory growth rate of enterprises

Second, the monetary policy was further loosened. Since the start of 2015, there have been 5 interest rate cuts and 5 bank reserve cuts. At the same time, by using PSL, SLF, MLF and policy instruments such as public market operation, the downward trend of loans in 2014 had been reversed. The weighted average profits of one-year interbank rates decreased from 5.26% in March of 2015 to 3.85% in August. The new Renminbi loans from January to September was 8992.29 billion yuan, increased by 1309.11 billion yuan than the same period of 2014. The balance growth rate of Renminbi loans reached 17.04%, 11.5% higher than the same period of 2014. The cumulative growth rate of social financing increased from -20.4% in the period from January to April of 2015 to -7.7% in the period from January to September with a rise of 12.7%.

Third, by using measures such as financial supervision, the positive financial policy has been implemented comprehensively. The positive fiscal policy set up at the beginning of 2015 was to raise up the fiscal deficit from 2.1% to 2.3%, and issue a local government bond of 600 billion yuan. However, up to now, due to the facts that carryover of the funds from 2014 was expedited, the issuance of special bonds by local governments and the promotion of debt exchange in local governments (a new bond of 600 billion yuan was issued by local governments, and a 3200 billion yuan worth debt exchange.) , the actual fiscal deficit was above 2.5% (the cumulative deficit was 5.5% from January to September). Meanwhile, the central government used development-oriented finance to make up for the fiscal gap and absence, speeding up financial allocation and strengthening the role of positive fiscal policy.

Fourth, real estate policy was adjusted in a large scale and the demand for self-use and improvement-based housing was encouraged by measures such as overall reduction on restrictions of house purchasing, loaning, business tax, and turning government-purchased houses into affordable houses.

Fifth, the burden on enterprises was reduced substantially by streamlining the government, allocating power to lower levels and using various kinds of structural burden-reduction measures. For example, 12 charges on enterprises was canceled or suspended, and 47 charges on small and medium-sized enterprises. All these measures will relieve a burden of more than 40 billion yuan annually from enterprises; more than 600 charges were canceled, suspended or reduced, including administrative charges and government funds, reducing the burden on enterprises by more than 100 billion yuan; The new policy on asset depreciation promulgated by the state council

Could reduce 233.3 billion yuan for the enterprises of A share in the first year. In addition, the five interest rates cutting also made the lending rates largely lower for enterprises, which saved the enterprise plenty of expenditures on interest rates.

Sixth, the slackness of governance existing in some regions started to be reversed by political accountability and administrative supervision.

Seventh, the policies encouraging entrepreneurship and innovation was implemented in a large scale, and the support for emerging strategic industries has been further strengthened.

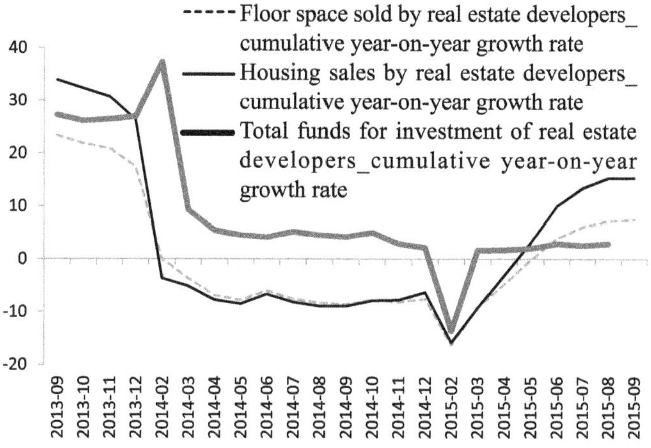

Figure 2-36 Signs of real estate market pick-up

These policies has worked to a certain extent. For example, a string of policy easing has reversed the downward trend of real estate sales, and the bottoming of real estate market became increasingly clear. From January to September, accumulated sales of real estate floor space rose by 7.5% year-on-year, and the sales grew by 15.3%, respectively a 16.1% and 24.2% increase compared with the same period in 2014, and also 3.6% and 5.3% higher than the first half of the year. The recovery of real estate sales directly resulted in the reverse of real estate funds outflow. From January to August, thc cumulativc fund growth rate of real estate developers was 2.8%, 1.2% higher than that from January to March, and maintained at the same level as that from January to June, which means that the fund for real estate fund development remained stable. This led to the rise of investment in some regions, particularly for the first tier cities.

However, on the whole, the current policies and measures has not brought about overall and stable recovery. First, the slow-down of industry did not have any obvious pick-up. On the contrary, recently there was even a slight decline of PMI. In October, PMI was 49.8%, lower than 50 for three consecutive months. In a longer term, PMI has been fluctuated around 50 for as long as 4 years, which meant that in a short time it was difficult for the manufacturing industry to recover.

Second, the downward trend of investment in both manufacturing industry and real estate has not been reversed, and investment demand has been decreasing rapidly. From January to September, the cumulative growth rate of asset investment was 8.3%, 5.8% lower than the same period in 2014, among which the growth rate of manufacture investment was 8.3%, 5.5% lower than the same period in 2014; the growth rate of real estate investment was 3.8%, 8.8% lower than the same period in 2014. In 2015, in general terms the Chinese economy was declining affected by both factors with a trend and factors with seasonality, with obvious downturn in all kinds of macro-indicators, which was beyond the expectation of market and showed signs of a new round of recession. General speaking, in 2015 the economy only had pick-ups in some local areas, and the bottoming of economy in a short term began to show up. However, whether the macro-economy would be able to recover stably as a whole is still depends on the solidity of economic foundation.

3. 2016 in the Process of Heading for Bottom

2016 will be the year when the Chinese economy will be heading for the bottom in a all-round way. On one hand, it will follow the basic logic behind the new normal state with all kinds of macro-economic indicators going down affected by both factors with a trend a factors with seasonality; on the other hand, with the promotion of internal structure adjustment, the formation of new driving mechanism for economic growth and the marginal improvements of external environment, the Chinese economy will maintain stable during its process of heading for the bottom in 2016. The Chinese economy will witness a continuous downward in the first and second quarter of 2016, and will stumble across a painful period of hitting the bottom in the third quarter. After that, the economy will show signs of being relatively stable. In 2016, there are two major risks and four imperative issues that need our attention.

3.1. The basic logic and forecast for the economic bottom

The bottom of the Chinese economy are the joint products of manifold cyclic forces. It is not only determined by the stableness of medium and long-term factors with a trend; more importantly, it is also decided by the time when various kinds of cyclic forces hit the bottom and the way the economy operate at the bottom. Will the world economy have a double-dip recession in 2016? Will there be a successful reversion in the downward real estate investment in the second quarter of 2016? Can the debt restructuring in China relieve the pressure on enterprises? Can China launch its stock adjustment in a large scale? Is the incremental expansion enough to fill up the gap made by the unbalanced reversal and traditional stock adjustment? Can the re-orientation of macro-economic policy effectively change the pessimistic expectation of actors at micro-level, and effectively prevent the "deflation-debt effect" from being prominent? Could the motivation mechanism for incentive compatibility be efficiently established in this round of large-scale reform and adjustment? All these factors will together determine the bottom of the Chinese economy as well as its depth and length of persistence.

The research findings of our team at the second quarter of 2015 said:" From the cyclical perspective, the year of 2015 will not be the second bottom of the 'asymmetric W' , which illustrated the cyclical adjustment. The world economic cycle, the Chinese real estate cycle, the debt cycle, the inventory cycle, the new industries cycle as well as the political cycle together determines that a strong recovery will not happen until the second half of 2016." The logic behind this conclusion is still valid. However, considering the facts such as possible deviations to the world economy in 2016, the strong effects brought by the stock market crash to the third and fourth quarter of 2015, the re-orientation of various kinds of policies after the The fifth Plenary Session of the 18th CPC Central Committee, we partially revised the arrival time and length of persistence of the Chinese economic bottom, i.e. the Chinese economy will still be on its way heading to the bottom, and will show signs of keeping stable at the end of the year. The length of this round of economic operation at the bottom will last for around 1 year, and from the second half of 2016 to the beginning of 2018 the macro-economy will gradually recovering.

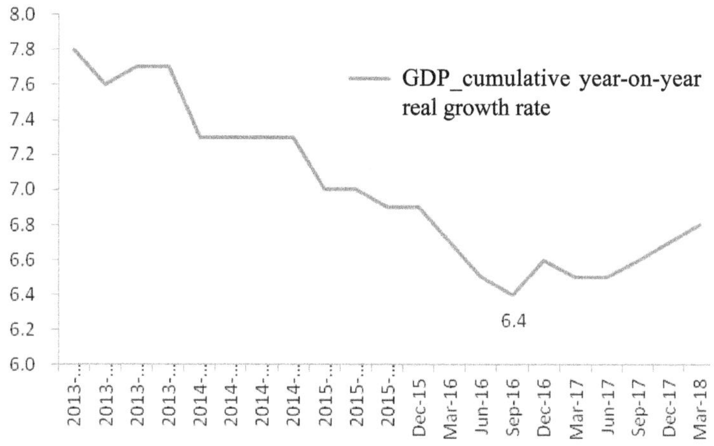

Figure 3-1 Prediction of China's GDP in future

(1) The general reversion of the world economy will alleviate China's external imbalance and internal overcapacity . Before the bottom of the world economy shows up, it is hard for the Chinese economy to bottom out.

There are several critical criteria by which we indentify the bottom of the world economy.

First, the core reason for the world economic crisis – global imbalance, has been basically solved, and the external imbalance of major economies remain in a stable state. However, judging from the current data, this imbalance is not at the bottom with a relative stable level. According to the forecast by IMF, China's external imbalance will continue, and the imbalance of the emerging economies is expanding. The trade deficit is still at the bottom level, which will continue to be like this for the 5 years ahead. Among them, the share that Chinese trade surplus takes up in DGP will go down from 3.1% in 2015 to 0.6% in 2020, and the share that American trade surplus takes up in GDP will increase from -2.6% to -3.4%.

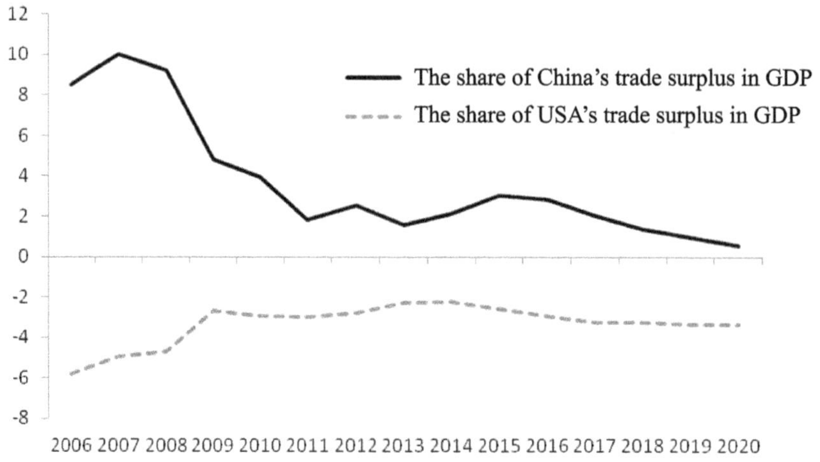

Figure 3-2 Imbalanced reversion is still ongoing

Second, the demand for bulk commodity bottoms out, indicated by the fact that the price of bulk commodity has already recovered getting rid of the downward trend of commodity super cycle. For the time being, although the price of bulk commodity dropped down substantially in 2015, due to the factors such as weak demand, overload inventory and disordered competition of supply, the price of bulk commodity will drop down slightly in 2016. According to the forecast put forth by IMF, the world bulk commodity index was 112 in 2015, 59% lower than that of 2014. The bulk commodity index in 2016 will be 108, even 4% lower than that of 2015. There will be a slight pick up of bulk commodity index to 113. Therefore, we can tell from the changing trajectory of bulk commodity that the global manufacture will still in recession.

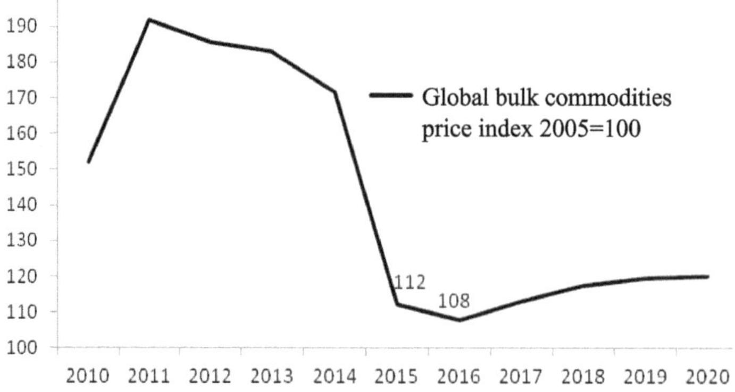

Figure 3-3 Global bulk commodities price almost hit the bottom

Third, the spreading of global economic crisis has ended, which means that there will not be further downward demand or large-scale financial upheavals, and the relative exchange rate of all kinds of currencies will maintain stable. According the theory on the global economic crisis spreading, the current economic crisis has not ended. The root reason for this are: (1) the large volatilities for emerging economies are just beginning; (2) the adjustment of global real economy was much lag behind the adjustment of financial sectors, the big adjustment of investment in real economy brought by unbalanced reversion has not been carried out in all round way; particularly, the adjustment of balance sheet of manufacture and raw material industries in emerging economies is just beginning; (3) it is still much too early for a general exit from all kinds of bailout measures for the stock market.

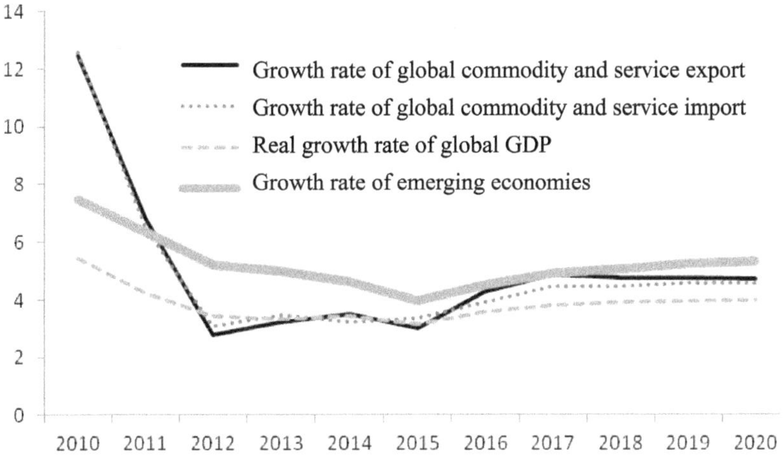

Figure 3-4 Spreading of global economy cycles

Although many existing forecasts are keen to believe that 2015 will be the lowest point of the world economy in this round, they are more like bright anticipations which work as the guide for public expectation. At the same time, these forecasts only considered the general situation without fully thinking about plenty of uncertainties and potential risks. Judging from current data and research theories, we have to carefully consider the following four issues:

First, the normalization of the American monetary policy, the further downturn of the demand of Chinese import, the further decrease of international bulky commodity , as well as the prominent problem caused by the early mismatch of manufacture industry – these all determined that the turbulences facing with the emerging economies in 2016 might surpass all other volatilities the emerging economies had in the past.

Second, the challenges beyond expectation caused by all kinds of geopolitics might sabotage the recovery of European economy. For example, the spiraling refugee problem in Europe might sparkled strong nationalism, which further endangered the cohesion of Europe. The UK might want to leave the EU in 2016 or 2017, which will compound the disintegration of the EU. Meanwhile, the terrorist event in Paris was likely to make Europe to deploy more conservative policies, which might lead to the result that the QE policy in Europe would not achieve the expected goal.

Third, the global investment and trade contraction was not over. The world macro-economy not only lacks unified policy coordination at macro-level, but also in more shortage of the foundation for economic recovery and fundamentals for mid-term prosperity.

Fourth, the spreading mechanism of the world economic crisis determines that the spreading of this round of crisis from financial sectors to real economy, and from the core to the peripheral has not been over yet. The adjustment of the balance sheet of emerging economies was just beginning. Hence, the world economy not only faces with a state of continuous slow-down, but was also confronted with the possibility of double-dip recession. This means that China will not only face with constant challenges brought by the world trade contraction, but also challenged by the global capital fluctuations. It will be very difficult for the Chinese economy to realize cyclic reversion before the world economy hits its bottom. Therefore, the time from 2015 to 2016 will be the bottom of the world economy, which determines that the Chinese economy will hit its bottom from 2016 to 2017.

(2) Substantial implementation of overcapacity reduction is the second largest factor that determines the bottom of the Chinese economy. If the “Zombie enterprises”, the enterprises with high debt and in the industries with overcapacity will not be adjusted comprehensively under the forces of market and administration, it will be difficult for the

Chinese economy to bottom out.

According to the current data, affected by external unbalanced reversion in large scale and rapidly declining internal demand, the Chinese economy has already begun to make adjustments. However, this adjustment has mainly focused on inventory and some business conducts. The substantial adjustments such as bankruptcy, merger, and debt restructuring has not been carried out in a all-round way. A large quantity of enterprises with asset liability ratio of more than 100% are still in operation. The local governments and banks are still subsidize and advance to those enterprises with large deficits. A large number of bad loans are still covered by extension period and "borrowing new loans to repay the old debt". For instance, the overall asset liability ratio of the steel industry was more than 70%, and 80% of the enterprises had large deficits. However, the year-on-year steel production was not less from January to October of 2015, only with its growth rate declining from 11% to 1% for the time being.

However, if we look at all kinds of performance-related parameters, we can see that China has already entered a time-window for the large-scale inventory adjustments.

The major sign for this is that the industrial profits declined rapidly in the five areas of China which had been severely stricken by recession, which resulted in a one-year negative growth of the overall industrial enterprises, particularly for the state-owned enterprises with a decrease rate as high as 30%. Therefore, we saw a half-year negative growth in industries such as cement and glass for the fist time over the past 20 years in 2015.Among them, the year-on-year growth rate of cement was -4.8%, and the same of plate glass was -8.3%. If we consider the measures of inventory adjustment and supply-side reform put forth by the The fifth Plenary Session of the 18th CPC Central Committee, we could say that the government will actively promote the adjustments of "zombie enterprises", enterprises with high debts and overcapacity. We could also estimate that the bottom of overcapacity reduction will be seen in an acceleratory way, probably in the second half of 2016 or the first half of 2017. The release of market space and the restoration of functions of economic operational channel will lay a solid foundation for the Chinese economy to bottom out in the second half of 2017.

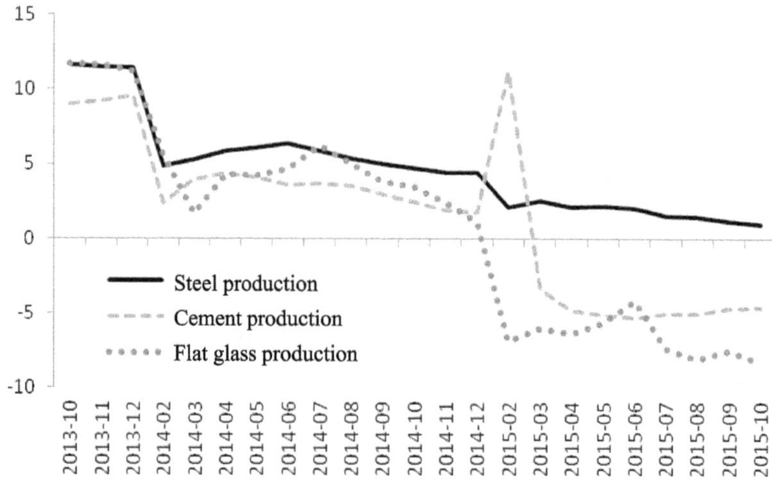

Figure 3-5 Differentiation during de-capacity of industries with overcapacity

(3) judging from the current inventory cycle, the time from 2014 to 2015 was the downward period of this round of inventory cycle. Because of the high debt rate, market price deflation and shrinking expected profits of investment, many enterprises take "cash is king" as their business strategy, which reduced inventory investment as much as possible. The growth rate of the capital tied up by enterprise stock is not only continuously decreasing, but also much lower than that of enterprise finished product. According to the current calculation, this round of stock will bottom out around the first quarter of 2016.

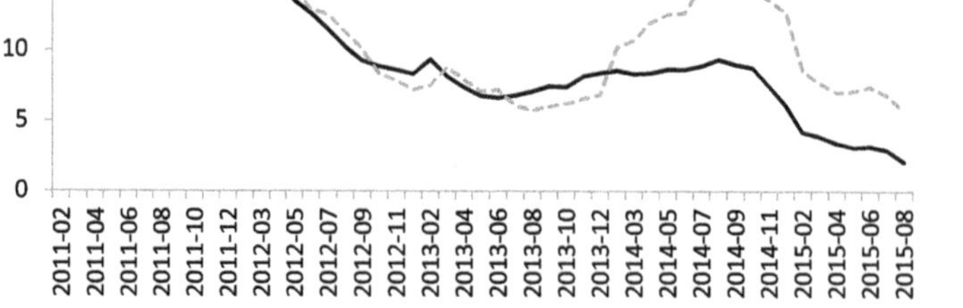

Figure 3-6 Inventory cycle is on downward stage

(4) The real estate cycle still makes a great contribution to the Chinese economy, therefore the bottom and length of persistence of real estate investment will also strongly affect the bottom of length of persistence of macro-economy.

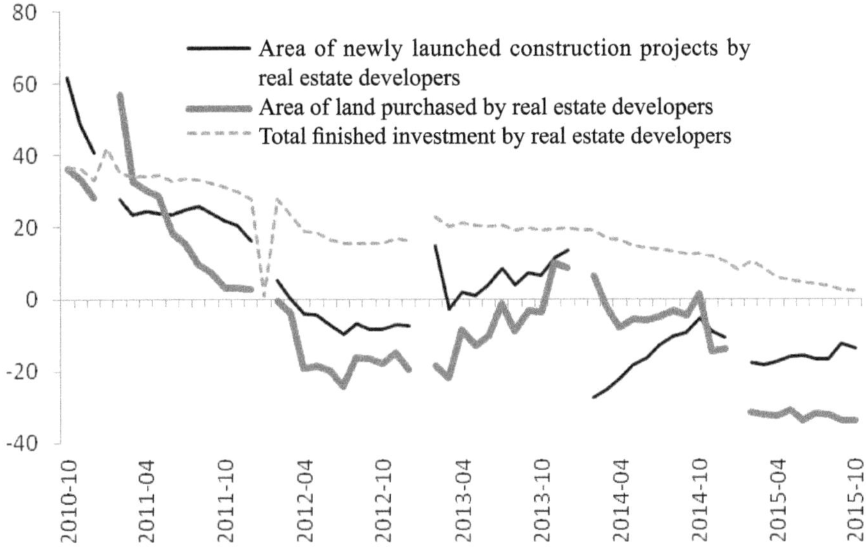

Figure 3-7 The pick-up of downward growth rate of real estate investment was not obvious

For the time being, the real estate investment still takes up 18% of the overall investment in China. Meanwhile, the real estate investment will affect the production and investment in 18 industries through industrial chain. Hence, the bottom of real estate investment is one of the leading reference points for judging the bottom of the Chinese macro-economy. According to the spreading rule of real estate indicator from past experience, 2-3 quarters after the data of real estate sales and price turning into positive, the date of real estate investment will recover. However, judging from current situation, this spreading period will be extended due to the impacts from the following factors: first, China's large stock of houses have a strong impact on the inflow of capitals from real estate developers; second, the disappearance of demographic dividend in China strong affected the investment expectation of real estate developers; third, the connection between traditional real estate developers and government officials was shattered in the anti-corruption campaign, and the competition model has changed. Fourth, excessive regional differentiation made the adjustment cycle of China's real estate industry longer and riskier than before. Therefore, we can tell from the date that the growth rate of real estate sales from April to May of 2015 rose up, yet the growth rate of real estate investment declined from 10.5% at the beginning of 2015 to 2% in October. More importantly, the new construction areas declined 13.9% year-on-year from January to October, and area of purchased land declined 33.8% year-on-year. This was a sign of a continue drop of real estate growth rate in a short period of time. For the time being, it is estimated that the growth rate of real estate investment will be back to around -4%,and will stop to drop further in the second quarter. It will also recover in a noticeable way after various kinds of real estate stock reduction and support policies are introduced and implemented by different regions of China.

(5) in the process when the new structure replacing the old one, the development situation determines the foundation for and the nature of China's economic recovery. The development of emerging industries is supported mainly by two forces. First, the rise of market demand brought by the adjustment of relative price. This is the most persistent force that makes the emerging industries to develop tremendously. Since 2008, China' s economic imbalance has been reversing, and all kinds of relative price parameters have gone through major adjustments. For instance, the trade condition turned from less than 1 in 2011 into more than 1, and began to rapidly rise up since 2014 with a growth rate of around 15%; take another example, the relative prices of industrial products and service products went down quickly from the highest point of 1.05 to 0.99 now. This directly resulted in the prosperity of service industries. Therefore, it has been four years since China started the market-oriented industrial transition. Meanwhile, the policy support provided by the government to the public services, strategic emerging industries, innovation and entrepreneurship also have boosted the development of emerging industries. But it must be admitted that it is difficult for these emerging industries to completely substitute the growth momentum of traditional industries and work as the new key industries which can lead China's economic growth in short term. In fact, many measures of policy support will face with the leftover from over-stimulation in the

future. Therefore, in 2016 it will be difficult for emerging industries and new force to prevent the traditional industries from pulling the Chinese economy down to the bottom.

(6) The debt cycle is the most direct force that determines the cycle of this round of Chinese economic performance. The stock market disaster from June to July of 2015 fueled the rising of China's debt ratio. The overall restart of IPO in 2016, the rapid local debt replacement and the bad assets stripping and disposal will directly decides the performance of Chinese debt cycle.

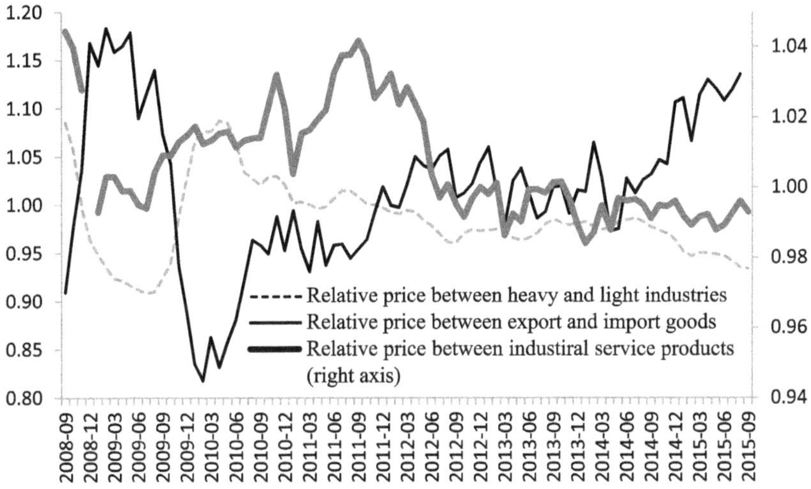

Figure 3-8 Significant adjustments of various kind of relative price indexes

Just as our research team pointed out, the stock market disaster in 2015 made China's debt problem even worse, and at the same time impeded China's leverage reduction and assets replacement. This brought difficulties to us to change China's financial structure by the means such as debt to equity swap for the sake of reducing the pressure on enterprises. In the third and fourth quarter of 2015, China was forced to carry out debt financing again, which would boost the rise of debt in 2016. It is estimated that the debt needed to be repaid will account for 17% of GPD, and the overall debt ratio will be more than 260%. The combination of high debt ratio and enterprise debt ratio will make the Chinese economy to decline more rapidly, put off the time when the Chinese economy hits the bottom, and make the Chinese economy to operation at the bottom for a longer period. Fortunately, the central government has paid much attention to the highly-indebted debt ratio and enterprise debt ratio with a series of steps dealing with this problem, such as the restarting of IPO, the restructuring of highly-indebted state-owned enterprises, the shattering of rigid repayment, the reduction of pressure on enterprise, the stripping of bad assets and capitalization of assets and further expansion of debt replacement scale, etc. Therefore, our conclusion is that the second quarter of 2016 will still be the most difficult time for China's capital and enterprises, and with all kinds of measures implemented for one quarter, the problem will be alleviated .

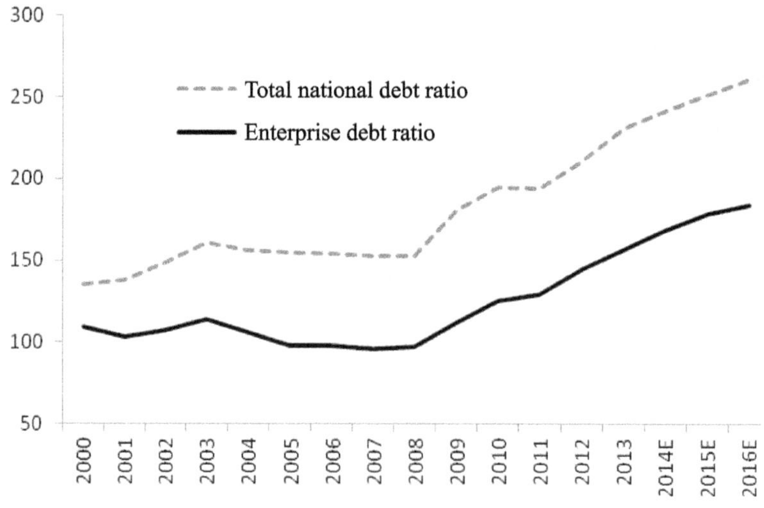

Figure 3-9 China's rising debt ratio

(7) The lack of incentive compatibility in the new round of large-scale reform and adjustment was the essential reason for the economic downward. Whether the re-orientation of large-scale reform and adjustment in 2016 will build up a new mechanism of incentive compatibility will be a critical factor responsible for the successful bottom-out of the Chinese economy.

According to the plan put forth by the Central Reform Leading Group, various kinds of reforms in China will be carried out comprehensively from 2015 to 2017. The year of 2016 will not only be a year in which the reform rolls out in a all-round way, but is also the first year of the 13th Five-Year Plan. After some progress has been made for the current stage in terms of anti-corruption movement, the campaign-like anti-corruption will turn into regulated and systematic supervision, which will provide the reformers with an valuable opportunity to re-evaluate the reform and re-think the next steps for further reform. Meanwhile, because the logic of "smash the old and set up the new" is still valid, the continuous decline of economy in 2016 will create conditions for the establishment of new power mechanism for reform. Based on this judgment, in 2017 the economy will have an obvious pick-up affected by new power mechanism and reform dividend.

Base on our understanding of the 7 aspects discussed above, we believe this round of mid-term adjustment will have its low point at the third quarter of 2016 with a growth rate of 6.4%. By the middle and late period of 2017 the Chinese economy will have a slight recovery; the output gap will be narrowed substantially; the growth rate of nominal GDP will maintain a stable pace, and there will be signs of easing economic policies.

According to the calculation of the forecast model, the real growth rate of GDP for the whole year of 2016 will be 6.6%, and the nominal growth rate of GDP will be 6.5%; the growth rate of consumption, investment and export will be respectively 10.5%, 9.6% and 2.1%; the growth rate of the primary, secondary and tertiary industries will be respectively 4.0%, 5.4% and 8.0%.

3.2. Two kinds of risks China will be confronted with in 2016

There will be great uncertainty for the Chinese macro-economy in 2016. This uncertainty stems from our knowledge about potential risks and our measures to tackle these risks. In our report of the fourth quarter of 2014, our focus were the following six issues: " business climate change in the service industry", " the deterioration of enterprise performance", "declining quality of employment", "roaring possibility of debt risks", "the adjustment on real estate cycles" and "failure of monetary policy" . In our report of the second quarter of 2015, we pointed out that the priorities are the following 4 issues: growth rate downturn and economic bottom, deflation-debt effects, macro-restructuring and overall inefficiency of macro-economic policy. In 2016, the risks listed above will still be existing, and will collide and interact with each other under the downward pressure. This will result in two kinds of risks in 2016: first, collective deviation of micro-economic actor behavior, which will encourage the endogenous downward force; second, the further concentration of "recessive bubbles", which will further distort the finance and enlarge regional risks.

(1) Pressured by declining profits expectation and expanding deficits as well as the "deflation-debt effect", the micro-economic actors' behavior deviated in a collective way, which has led to rapid economic shrinking and a deeper bottom with longer period for the Chinese economy.

1). Overall decline of enterprise performance indicators

First, the enterprise profits dropped down in a all-round way. To start with, the profit growth of the industrial enterprises came into negative. From January to August of 2015, the total profits of the industrial enterprises above designated size decreased by 1.9% on a year-on-year basis.The growth rate was 11.9% lower than the same period in 2014, and 15.5% lower than the same period of 2013. Among them, the state-owned enterprises experienced big slump. From January to September of 2015, the total profits of the state-owned enterprises decreased by 24.7%; the growth rate was respectively 30.0% lower than 2014 and 32.7% lower than 2013 (as shown in Figure 3 -10). Second, the growth rate of the listed enterprise profits also went down continuously to nearly zero. In the third quarter of 2015, the growth rate of the listed enterprise profits was only 0.4%, 8.4% lower than the same period in 2014 and 14.2% lower than the same period in 2013; the growth rate of the net profits of stakeholders attributable to parent company was 1.5%, 7.6% lower than the same period in 2014 and 12.9% lower than the same period in 2013.

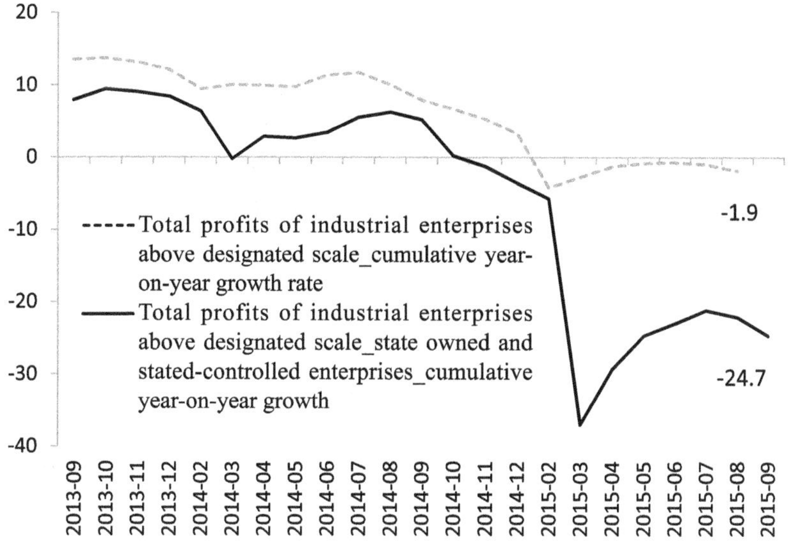

Figure 3-10 Negative growth of industrial enterprise profits

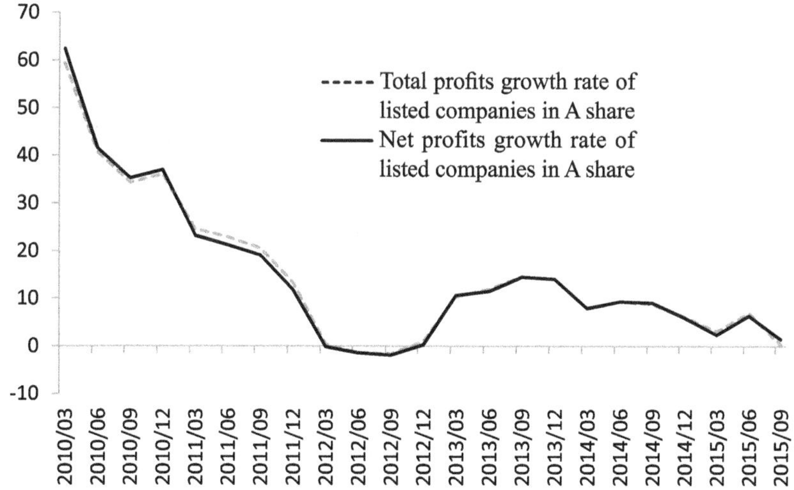

Figure 3-11 Zero profits growth of listed companies

Second, the enterprise deficits has been in a trend of expansion. From January to August of 2015, the number of loss-making enterprises above designated size increased by 13.6% on a year-on-year basis; the growth rate was respectively 10.5% higher than the same period in 2014 and 11.6% higher than the same period in 2013. Comparatively speaking, the total deficits of the loss-making enterprise increased more substantially with a growth of 22.8% from January to August, 12.9% higher than the same period in 2014 and 31.0% higher than the same period in 2013. The state-owned enterprises experiences more intense change. From January to September, the total deficits increased by 34.7% on a year-on-year basis, 24.5% higher than the same period in 2014 and 51.7% higher than the same period in 2013.

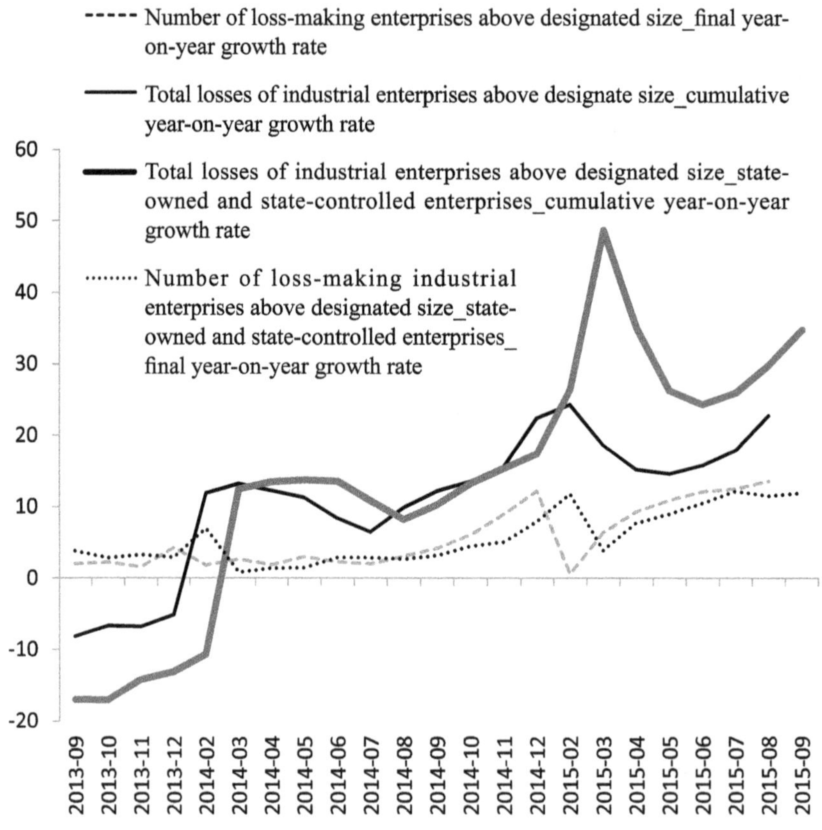

Figure 3-12 Area of loss-making was expanding

2). A new stage for the enterprise debts

The problem of enterprise debts entered into a new stage in the process of incessant rising. It dose not only evolved from "borrow loans for investment" model to "borrow new loans to repay the old" model, but more importantly some enterprise have already fully embraced "borrow new loans to pay the interest" model. The Chinese economy might be in the eve of balance sheet recession. As the date showed, the enterprise debts accounted for more than 178% of GDP, and the interest that enterprises have to pay took up more than 11% of GDP and around 60% of new bank loans. Some enterprises had to sell assets to repay their debts. This might undermine the stability of all kinds of capital markets at any time.

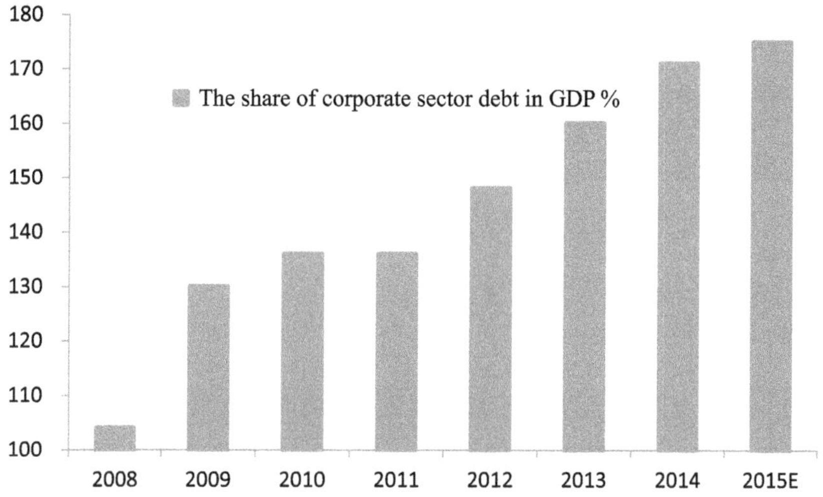

Figure 3-13 Roaring corporate sector debt

The cycle of debt stocks in enterprises consumed a large amount of capital, which made enterprises begin to borrow new loans to pay for the interest. The new investment has been curbed due to the shortage of capital. Although the enterprises have issued more and more credit debts since 2008, at the same time the capital used to repay the loans and interest was increasing year by year. In addition, with the escalation of debt level, the share of the capital used to repay the loans and interest has been expanding in the newly issued debt. The share of enterprise credit debt issued for repaying loans and interest in the total issued debts increased from 42% in 2008 to nealy 60% in 2014. In September of 2015, this ratio moved up further to 63%. A large amount of new capital was used to repay the old debts, which reduced the capital for new investment and affected the investment and operation of enterprises.

Rapidly increasing debts and excessive enterprise debt also intertwined with the deflation in manufacturing, which resulted in "deflation-high debts effects". The regional risk deterioration and spreading could be intensified anytime. The endogenous contraction will be more severe. The combination of deflation and high debts in manufacturing will directly lead to the roaring of actual cost for enterprises. For manufacture enterprises, the weighted interest rate of enterprise debts at the beginning of 2015 was around 8%. Although there have been five times of interest rate cuts, which reduced the financial cost by 100%, but the sale price of enterprises is declining.

3). Enterprises showed signs of behavioral deviation

First, pressured by return indicator and price indicator, the expected investment return declined substantially, which resulted in the shrinking of the endogenous investment demand. Currently there is significant slump in the growth rate of stock investment, loan financing and production expansion. The appearance of this deflationary effect will generate strong positive feedbacks, which will result in the increase of cumulative debt rate and growing of spillover effect. For example, because the biggest impact caused by deflation is targeted at future finance rather than current finance, in an environment of highly-indebted enterprise, deflationary market price and declining investment return, many enterprises adopted the strategy of "Cash is king" to minimize the stock investment as much as possible. In this situation, the growth rate of the enterprise stock investment was not only declined, but also significantly slower than that of the finished products. From January to August of 2015, the grow rate of stock funds in the enterprises above designated size was 2.1%, 7.2% lower than the same period of 2014; the year-on-year growth rate of account receivable decreased by 3.3%, and the year-on-year growth rate of finished products of the industrial enterprises was 5.7%, 9.9% lower than the same period of 2014. These data indicated that the "investment – stock – sales arrear" model, or the accelerator for cyclical fluctuation, is already counterproductive.

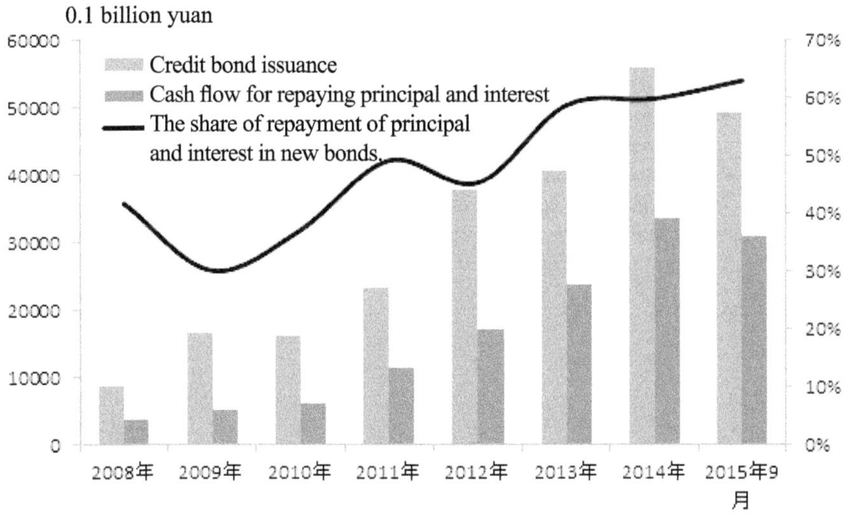

Figure 3-14 Enterprises borrow new loans to repay interest in an all-round way

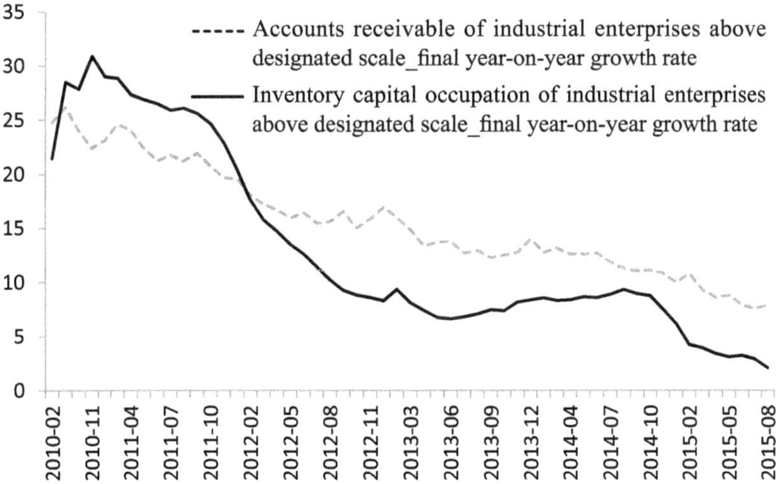

Figure 3-15 Endogenous contraction of enterprises were more and more explicit

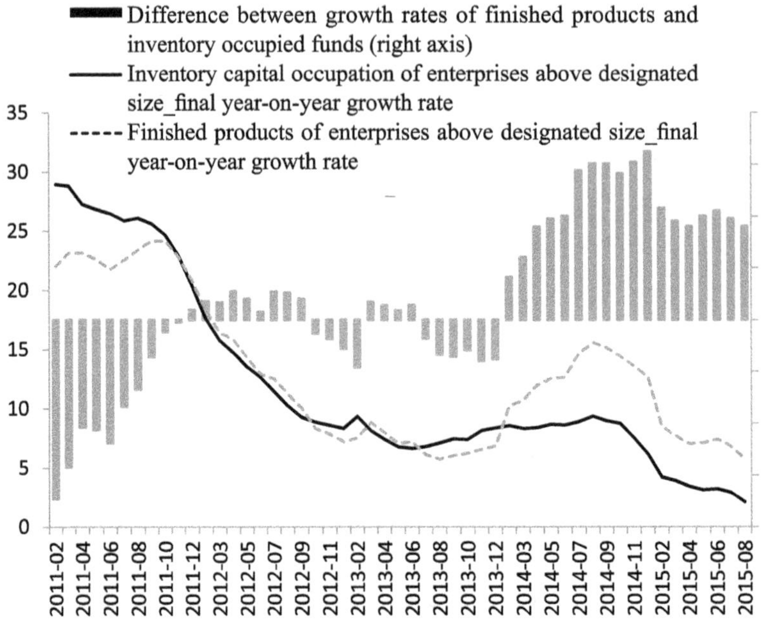

Figure 3-16 Endogenous contraction of enterprises were more and more explicit

Second, the Chinese enterprises began to borrow new loans to repay old debts instead of for investment, like they did in the past. Some enterprises even started to paying their interest on new loans. The Chinese economy might be on the eve of balance-sheet recession. This change was mainly reflected in the following two aspects. (as shown in Figure 3-17).

The first aspect was the fact that the enterprise asset and the growth rate of debts had significant declined. Moreover, during the process in which the enterprise assets growth are declining, the decrease of liquid assets and debts growth rate was larger than that of the total assets, and the growth rate, which in the past was higher or equal to that of the total assets, was significantly lower than that of the total assets.

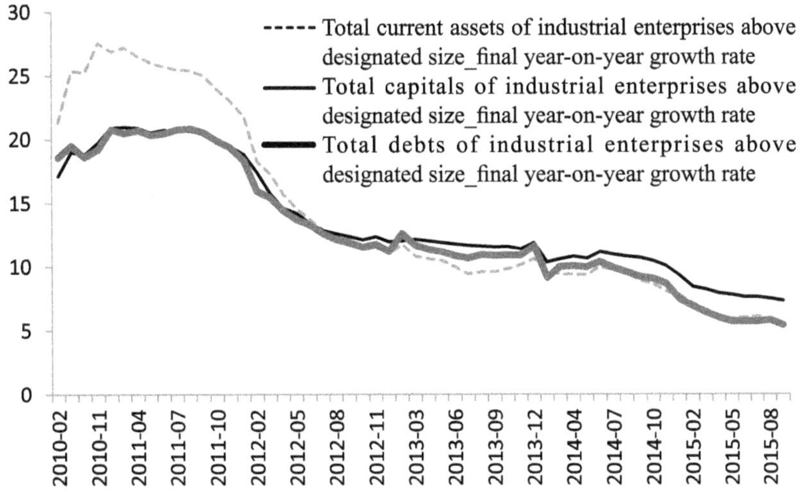

Figure 3-17 Significant decrease of enterprise assets and the growth rate of debts

The second aspect was the fact that the contraction of balance sheets of some industries had already happened. For example, the total assets of mechanic manufacture had its first negative growth of 0.54% at the second quarter of 2015. The negative growth went further to 0.65%, and the shareholders' equity had its first negative growth of 4.3%. This meant that the machinery manufacturing industry had entered into the state of asset contraction at the second quarter of 2015, and began to sell off their assets to repay their debts. This phenomenon also existed in the steel industry. In the third quarter of 2015, the total assets of the steel industry decreased by 1.12%, and the shareholders' equity decreased substantially by 13.72%. it could be seen that in the steel industry the phenomenon that a large amount of assets were sold for repaying debts began to emerge.

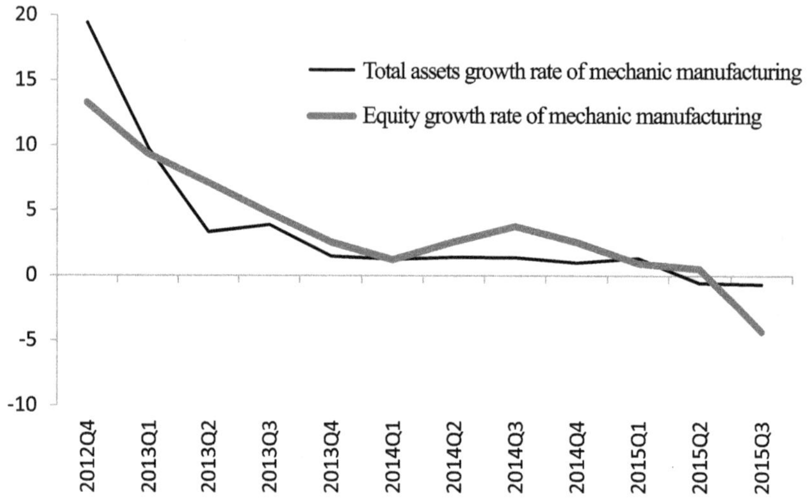

Figure 3-18 The balance sheet of mechanic manufacturing has started to shrink

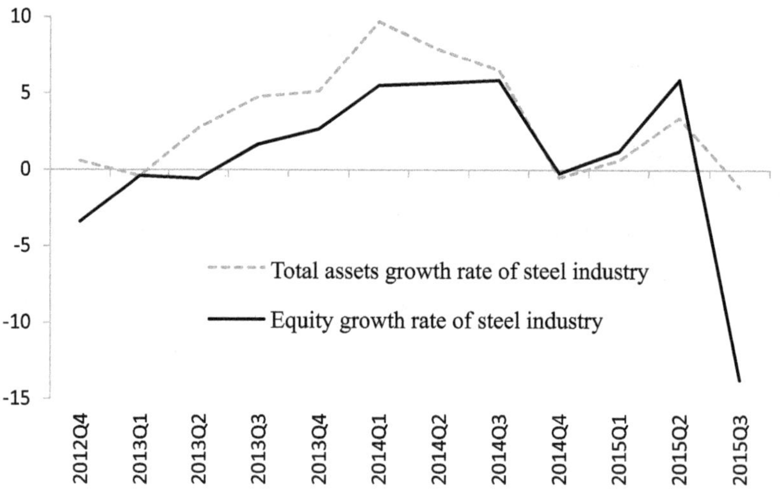

Figure 3-19 The balance sheet of steel industry has began to shrink

The third aspects was the fact that enterprises' demand for workers declined with mass layoffs, even with bankruptcy. With constant decline of economic growth, the industries with overcapacity and some traditional industries have been experiencing increasing difficulties in their business operation, and have gone to the brink of bankruptcy.

For example, since the first half of 2015, many large-scale textile and garment enterprises have gone into bankruptcy one by one. Some well-known textile and garment enterprises, such as Zhejiang Hongen Group Ltd., Wenzhou Judger Garment Co. Ltd. , Shandong Lanyan Co. Ltd., Zhejiang Wuyang Printing and Dyeing Co.Ltd., Dongguan Houhong Garment Co. Ltd., Alion Garment Co.Ltd., Baolijia Textile Co. Ltd. and Viscap Garment Co. Ltd., etc. All of these enterprises once had thousands of workers, but went into bankruptcy one by one since the second quarter of 2015 due to the difficulties in business operation, which led to mass layoffs. Although some state-owned enterprises are still struggling at the brink of bankruptcy. For instance, Hellongjiang Longmay Mining Holding Group Co.,Ltd., which had a staff of 233000, is currently faced with operational difficulties and significant losses. By this June, it owned its employees a total of 1.31 billion yuan in salary arrears and 2.27 billion yuan in other subsidies.

(II) Various kinds of "recessive bubbles" continued to gather, which led to further distortion of finance and expansion of regional risks.

With the Chinese economy entered into a time when the risks were concentrically released, all kinds of "recessive bubbles" crisis happened in succession. The financial risks was looming larger and larger during the transfer process, and the regional risks began to show signs of overall fragility of the Chinese economy. This was mainly reflected in the transfer process of "predicament of informal financing" → "roaring of interbank offered rate" → " debt default by enterprises such as Shanghai Chaori Solar Energy Science and Baoding Tianwei Group Co., Ltd. "→ "stock market crash" → " panic over exchange rates in August" . This indicated that the risks in Chinese economy had cumulated and been magnified during the transfer process, which finally became the flashpoint of the macro-economic deviation. When the Chinese economy is heading for the bottom in 2016, the effects of prevention, release and management of potential risks will determine when the Chinese economy will bottom out and how much it will recover.

Over recent years, the systemic risks of the Chinese economy and finance have accumulated and been released constantly. From time to time, the liquidity of capital from the real economy to financial sectors was embodied by different kinds of "recessive bubbles" with successive occurrences of bubble crisis, ranging from the informal credit crisis in Wehnzhou and Erdos, the city construction and investment bonds crisis from 2011 to 2012, the liquidity crisis of roaring interbank offered rate, the enterprise debt crisis such as Shanghai Chaori Solar Energy debt default, the crisis of Baoding Tianwei Group Co., Ltd. in the first half of 2016, the stock market crash happened in the middle of 2015, to the exchange rate panic in the second half of 2015. Each time the crisis generated certain degree of challenges to the market confidence and financial system. Besides, the occurrences of crisis have been more and more frequent. In such case, what will be the next potential risk in 2016? We think there are four aspects to which we should pay close attention:

Figure 3-20 Recessive bubble crisis happened one after another

1. Bond market bubble

After the blast of the stock market bubble, with the continuous decrease of stock price and suspension of IPO, the huge amount of capital gathered when the stock market was prosperous started to look for substitutes for investment. A large sum of capital flew into the bond market where new bubbles were taking shape. Since the June of 2015,the comprehensive net price index released by China Central Depository & Clearing Co., Ltd. (CCDC) have already ended its fluctuation over the past one year and increased continuously. Particularly, the issuance of cooperate bonds has increased exponentially with lower and lower issuing interest rate. From January to August of 2015, the Shanghai Stock Exchange have issued 514 enterprise bonds, the total volume issued was about 276. 25 billion yuan, a 56.7% increase comparing to the same period of 2014, and the total volume issued increased by 233.2%. Meanwhile, the issuance interest rates of enterprise debts were trading at record lows, even inconsistent with the state bonds. The coupon rate of enterprise bond in September on average was 4.54%, a 1.72% decrease than the same period in 2014. On the 18th of September, Shanghai Shimao Group successfully issued 5-year enterprise bonds of 6 billion yuan, whose coupon rate was only 3.9%; on the 25th of September, China Vanke Co., Ltd. issued 5-year enterprise bonds of 5 billion yuan, whose coupon rate was only 3.5%, which was a record low.

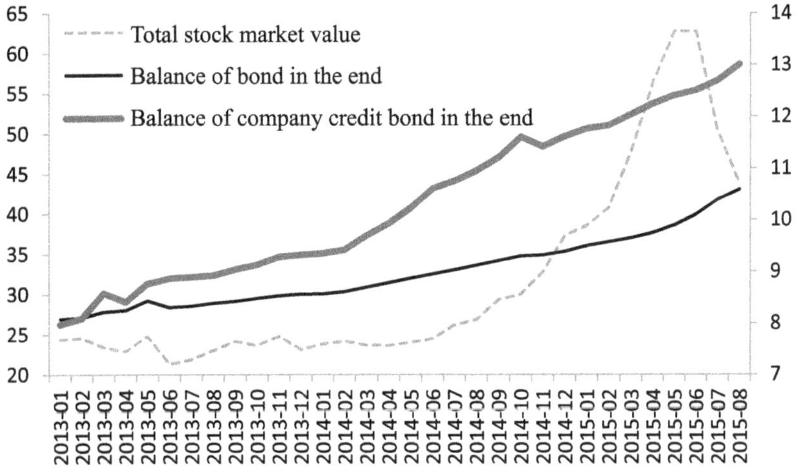

Figure 3-21 New bubbles was taking shape in bond market

In terms of the financial demand, because of the suspension of IPO and the relative decline of turnover on P2P platform, enterprises wanted to issue more bonds for financing. As one of the most important channel in which capital flew into the real economy, the good performance of the bond market during recent period had positive influence over the improvement of real economy to a certain degree. In terms of the capital supply, after the stock market bubble was popped, with the belief that the property market recovery would be weak and interest rate would go down, a large amount of speculative capital flew into the bond market for new items of investment. Therefore, new bubbles and market risks might be created.

Currently, the major risks existing in the market are high leverage rate, individual credit bonds default and lack of understanding towards risks. Due to the reason that stock exchange market allows impawn after warehousing, investors with institutions such as fund securities companies , in order to maximize their profits, will usually put on more leverage on credit bonds. Once the capital experiences abnormal turbulence, the investors will be forced to reduce leverage, which might lead to sell-offs of credit bonds. A recent report released by Commerzbank indicated that probability of substantial decline of bond market of China at the end of the year increased from almost zero in June to 20%. At the same time, there have been frequent enterprise debts defaults. Since the beginning of the third quarter, there have already been 3 instances of payment crisis related to enterprises of the Central Government. In September, China National Erzhong Group Co. and Baoding Tianwei Group Co. were all trapped in debt default, and so did Sinosteel in Octorber. More worrying is that up to now there haven't been any responses from the market, and there hasn't been significant spread between low credit rating and high credit rating bonds.

Therefore, how to properly deal with the outcome of the stock market bubble blast, to prevent new market bubbles and systemic risks from taking shape and to maintain relative operation of the stock market and bond market, has become one of the most important mission for micro-economic control at current stage.

2. Real estate bubble in regional areas

Since the April of 2015, affected by a series of easing-oriented policies, the real estate market have had significant recovery. Particularly in this June when the stock market bubble burst in a sudden, the central government introduced a series of easing-oriented policies which helped to create adequate liquidity. The large amount of funds gathered during the prosperous period of the stock market started to look for new investments in the real estate market. Massive speculative funds flew into real estate market of the first-tier cities, leading to formation of new bubbles.

Therefore, while the stock market was in a downturn, real estate market of the first-tier cities experienced “weak recovery” stimulated by a series of easing-oriented policies. Since this April, there has been significant recovery in property sales. The floor space sold and the sales figures were all stopped declining and began to rise on a year-on-year basis, with respectively cumulative growth of 7.5% and 15.3% from January to September, a 16.1% and 24.2% increased compared with the same period in 2014, and also a 3.6% and 5.3% increase compared with the first half of the year. Meanwhile, property price in more and more cities began to rise. Property price nationwide stopped declining and started to rise up since this April, and did so since August on a year-on-year basis. However, there were plenty of uncertainties in this round of real estate recovery. The largest risk would be that differentiation in the weak recovery might lead to serious “siphonic effect”, especially the substantial rise in property price in the first-tier cities will not only create regional bubbles, but also intensify regional difficulties and trigger systemic risks.

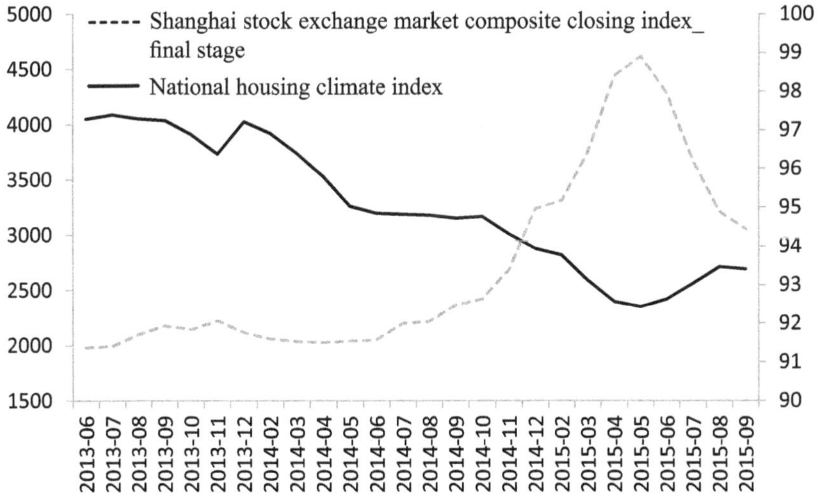

Figure 3-22 Alteration of real estate market and stock market climate

Against the backdrop of overall weak recovery, differentiation is enlarged in current real estate market. On one hand, the sales experienced substantial increase in first-tier cities such as Shenzhen and Beijing, etc.; on the other hand, there was constant decline of sales in the third and fourth cities. On one hand, performance of large-scale property enterprises has been improved comprehensively in the process of nationwide structural adjustment; on the other hand, performance of small property enterprises in the third and fourth-tier cities increasingly deteriorated. Although it is normal to have differentiation in recovery, compared with previous real estate recovery, the degree of differentiation we saw in this round of recovery was much larger than previous ones. This is the biggest threat to the prospect of recovery.

The intensification of market differentiation might lead to severe "siphonic effect": first, a large number of real estate enterprises will adjust their development strategies, accelerating various kinds of development funds flock into the first and second tier cities; the real estate market in the third and fourth-tier cities will continue to be in the downturn instead of following the recovery happened in the first and second-tier cities; third, the performance of large-scale property enterprises improved in the process of nationwide restructuring, while the small property developers will go to bankruptcy, and some financial difficulties at the county level will further worsen, which will trigger regional financial risks and social problems; fourth, under the situation in which the capital is in shortage and enterprises are highly indebted, the break of capital chain at individual points or emergence of financial risks will very likely lead to overall problem.

Therefore, the weak recovery with intensified differentiation contains plenty of uncertainties. We have to be aware that: first, rapid recovery in some regional areas will not necessarily generate "trickle-down effect". The skyrocketing property price is not good news for recovery. Second, the overall roaring of real estate market is not a target of micro-economic control. The damage brought by the new round of real estate bubble might be more severe than previous ones. Third, the skyrocketing property price in the first-tier cities under the situation in which the third and fourth-tier cities was in downward will not only trigger regional bubble, but also will make the real estate market in the third and fourth-tier cities to collapse through "siphonic effect", thus lead to overall problem.

3. Bubbles in the emerging strategic industries

The government-led innovation and entrepreneurship, the campaignstyle policy support and excessive subsidies as well as the lack of force from capital market to indentify risks existing in innovation – all of these are creating new bubbles in emerging strategic industries. However, China's social safety network for innovation and entrepreneurship has not been well established. There is a shortage of "cushion" against hard landing by those who failed in innovation and entrepreneurship. A cascade of bankruptcy which might occur after campaign-like innovation and entrepreneurship will have a major impact on socio-economy.

Some emerging strategic industries grew rapidly against all odds, but it is also important to note that behind this fast development there is a large amount of policy-related subsidies. Once these policy-related subsidies are removed, those enterprises will lack the capability for self-reliance. The establishment and fast development of some innovation-oriented enterprises were based on "story-telling" and "conceptual boast" instead of real market demand.

The burst of stock market bubble in 2015 had warned us of the bubble risks in emerging strategic industries, at the same time had produced major impacts on enterprises in these industries. Plenty of funds raised in the stock market flew into small and medium-sized enterprises and innovation-oriented enterprises through SME board and GEM. The collapse of stocks will start from SME board and GEM, which will not only make earlier investment and expansion by many enterprises become unfinished projects, but also generate too much debts for the innovative talents and weaken the confident of massive innovation and entrepreneurship.

Looking at the P/E ratio, we can see that there are still significant bubbles in the stock sectors of emerging strategic industries such as the A share of Shenzhen Stock Exchange, SME board and GEM. For instance, at the end of October the average P/E ration of Shenzhen Stock Exchange was 45.08, SME board 56.73, and GEM board 94.60. Although these figures were substantially lower than the record high in June 12th when the stock market crash occurred, they are much higher than their respective high points in the past. Their according annual returns also significantly lower than market risk-free rate of return, which was obviously inconsistent with performance of enterprises.

Table 3-1: P/E ration of stocks in related sectors of China's strategic emerging industries

Dates	A share of Shenzhen market(TTM)	Medium and small enterprises (TTM)	Growth enterprise market(TTM)
2015-10-30	45.08	56.73	94.60
2015-06-15 (Stock Market Disaster Day)	69.92	85.65	143.52
2014-12-31	35.94	42.59	63.76
2013-12-31	29.26	35.94	60.30
2012-12-31	26.97	28.33	34.35
2011-12-30	23.06	26.81	36.07
2010-12-31	39.67	48.99	70.75
2009-12-31	76.45	55.31	79.09
2008-12-31	17.57	21.91	
2007-12-28	58.32	68.59	
2006-12-29	51.67	39.95	
2005-12-30	34.92	21.69	
2004-12-31	27.16	31.36	

4. The volatilities of international financial market

From the point of view of future global economy and international capital market development, it is not only that global external demand will still be in downturn, but also that the financial volatilities with emerging economies as major actors and economic downward might further squeeze the space for the recovery of Chinese economy and become the next exposure point of China's macro-economic risks. Particularly, RMB exchange rate fluctuation and capital flights might be a critical element inducing new risks after the stock market crash.

In 2015, affected by expectation of interest increase by Federal

Reserve, a large amount of funds were on outflow, which had huge impacts on China's foreign exchange market and financial market. One important indicator used to monitor the situation is the balance of RMB counterpart of foreign exchange reserves. By the end of September of 2015, China's balance of RME counterpart of foreign exchange reserves was 27.400 billion yuan, 2000 billion yuan less than the balance of 29400 billion yuan at the end of 2014. Particularly since the exchange rate reform in August, the capital outflow has been increasingly faster. In August and September the RMB counterpart of foreign exchange respectively reduced.

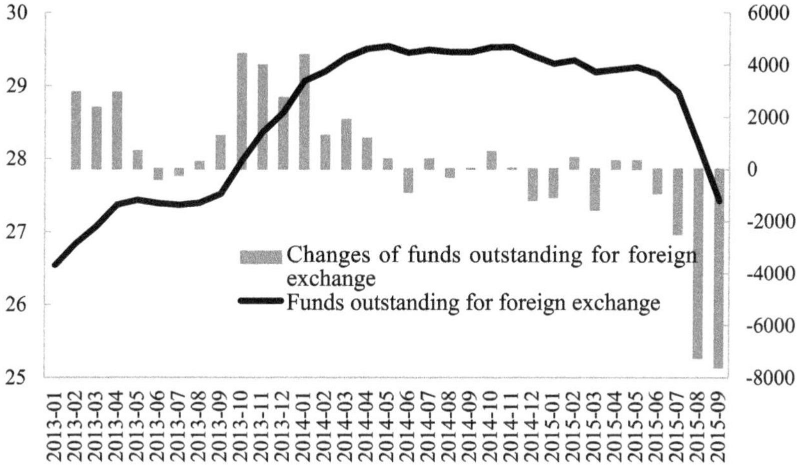

Figure 3-23 Sharp decrease of funds outstanding for foreign exchange

In addition, the outflow of capital also had adverse effects on China's enterprise credit. From January to September of 2015, the total social financing decreased by 7.7% compared with the same period in 2014. One of the important factors was the decrease of foreign currency loans. From January to September, foreign currency loans were -265.91 billion yuan, 641.51 billion yuan less than 375.6 billion yuan of the same period in 2014 with a decrease rate of 170.8%. This put extra pressure on enterprise credit and financing.

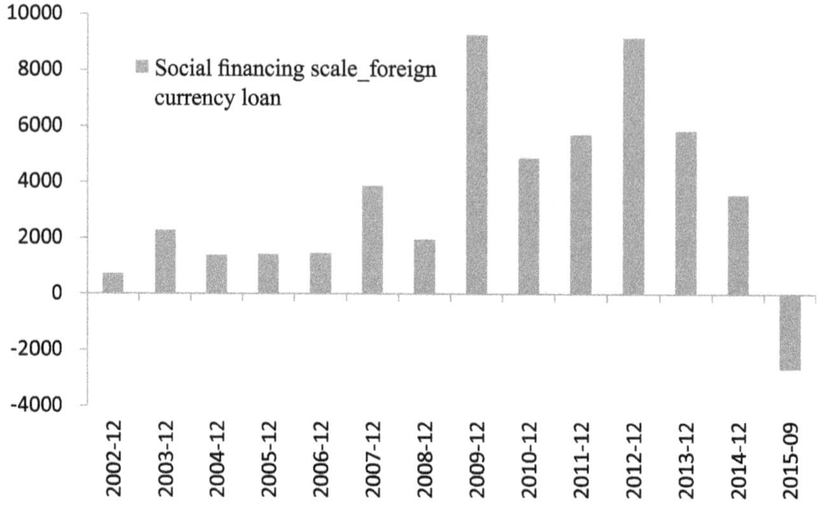

Figure 3-24 Foreign currency loan in social financing was dropping down substantially

Therefore, if international financial market experienced turbulences in 2016 and caused massive influx and outflow of capitals, it will become the next exposure point of Chinese macro-economic risks which would bring serious risks to stability of China's economic and financial system and further squeeze the space for Chinese economic recovery.

3.3. Four key issues in 2016

In 2016, there will be four key issues related to the two kinds of major risks aforementioned.

(1) whether or not the motivation mechanism of incentive compatibility in the new round of large-scale reform and adjustment will be well established. In 2016, the establishment of incentive system of interest compatibility will be in bad need. The most fundamental motivation incentive mechanism has been shattered, but a interest compatibility system of incentive mechanism, which are in line with the new normal state, have not been established; The anti-corruption campaign has blocked many illegitimate access to interest, but has not build up a legitimate motivation system very well; initiative of all levels of elites was fading away, and various kinds of traditional patterns of

compliance was broken. However, unanimous actions and good synergy have not been formed based on the mission of reform and adjustment for the new normal state. This was reflected in the following three aspects:

1. All levels of government officials, particularly the ones at local levels, showed increasing slackness in their work. The conventional governmental performance assessment system has been abolished, but new assessment and incentive system has not been established. Initiation and innovation of government in reforming substantially declined, and governments of all levels, which kept fiscal funds intact in their account, would prefer old routes of practices to breaking conventions and exploration. This resulted in shortage of promotion and implementation at local level for carrying out all kinds of macro-economic policies as well as overall malfunction.

Deviation of government behavior has made the fiscal policy supposed to be positive not positive with significant fiscal austerity. This has been specified in the following three aspects,

First, although investment put into government projects was always large in scale, it was a very slow process in which funds for projects was allocated and new constructions started. According to a report released by the National Audit Office, some key projects and wellbeing projects were slow in progress. (1) some key projects were slow in progress. 193 out of 815 projects audited (a share of 23.7%)were behind schedule with an investment of 286.86 billion yuan involved (a share of 40.5%). Among the ongoing 333 railway projects, the completion rates of annual investment plan of 99 projects were less than 50%, which involved 173.72 billion yuan; among them, the completion rates of annual investment plan of 20 projects were less than 10%. One completed project has not been put into use for 19 months, which caused an investment of 1.175 billion yuan to be without benefits. The central government invested 12.43 billion yuan into key water-saving agriculture projects of 2015 in 29 provinces, but the implementation was so slow that only 0.71 billion yuan was used. 7 national expressway network projects in 4 provinces which were supposed to began did not even started; some highway projects in 2 provinces were behind schedule. Some engineering projects of China Southern Power Grid, China Unicom, China Mobile and China Telecom were behind schedule. Besides, the Reform and

Development Commission was slower in approving projects which were attended to annually over the previous years. (2) Some wellbeing projects were not well implemented, and related projects had slow progress. In terms of affordable house construction, the projects in 11 provinces moved along at a slow pace. 12 counties, cities and institutions in 7 provinces made false reports that 14450 houses were started construction or completed. 57500 houses completed in 5 counties and cities of 5 provinces were not put into use. In terms of rural dilapidated building rennovation, the project starts were low, with some of the completed houses not being put into use or be used in other ways. In 2015, 2.453 million renovation projects out of a task of 4.32 million assigned by the central government started (a share of 56.8%).In 10 provinces, due to the reason of ill-preparation and delay of matching funds, the starts were less than 50%. Some areas of 3 provinces made false reports about starts rate, did not put completed houses into use or used them in other ways.

Second, the government expenditure is slowing down, particularly for the growth rate of local governmental expenditures. From January to September of 2015, the growth rate of national governmental expenditure was 15.1%, only 1.9% higher than the same period in 2014. Considering that the governmental expenditure on land grant, the growth rate of total expenditure was declining to a certain degree. In addition, the local governmental expenditure experienced larger decrease compared with the central government. From 2010 to 2013, the growth rate of local governmental expenditure was substantially higher than that of central government, and be basically flat with the latter in 2014. In 2015, the growth rate of local government was significantly lower than that of central government. From January to September of 2015, the growth rate of central governmental expenditure was 15.3%, 3.5% higher than the same period of 2014. The growth rate of local governmental expenditure was 15.0%, only 1.5% higher than the same period of 2014.

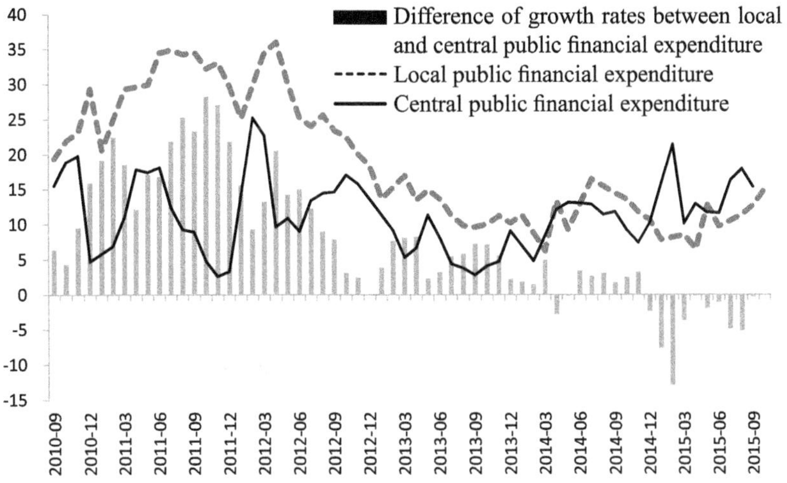

Figure 3-25 Large decrease of local government financial expenditure

Third, governmental saving was at high level. By the end of September in2015, governmental saving was 4110 billion yuan, 0.55% lower than the same period in 2014. Taking government organs and social groups into account, the total governmental saving reached 25040 billion yuan, 11.46% higher than the same period in 2014. Due to the reasons such as tighter financial supervision, financial appropriation and usage was slower than expected. According to the newest Announcement of Audit Finding, all governmental departments was slow in planning and spending public funds. After random inspection on wellbeing projects in fields such as agriculture and forest, poverty-lifting, social security and employment, urban and rural community affairs, affordable housing, aging-care, etc with 47.678 billion yuan financial funds, it is found that 14.176 billion yuan from 33 projects in 22 provinces were not efficiently utilized due to the reasons such as regulation restrictions, inconsistency between budget and implementation, long project approval time, ill-planned funds from completed projects, etc. some central institutions and local areas did not use financial savings in a completely and timely manner. For instance, subsidies from vehicle purchase tax on local construction projects had large amount of balance during carryover; Some special transfer payments in the governmental fund at central level and general public budget would wait for a long time to get approval. National tax system and Civil Aviation Administration of China did not clean up and revitalize their funds very well, and their previous annual balance was not turned into real expenditure, which became second-time residue. Some provinces such as Inner Mongolian Autonomous Region, did not revitalize fund very well, which resulted in a balance of 0.797 billion yuan.

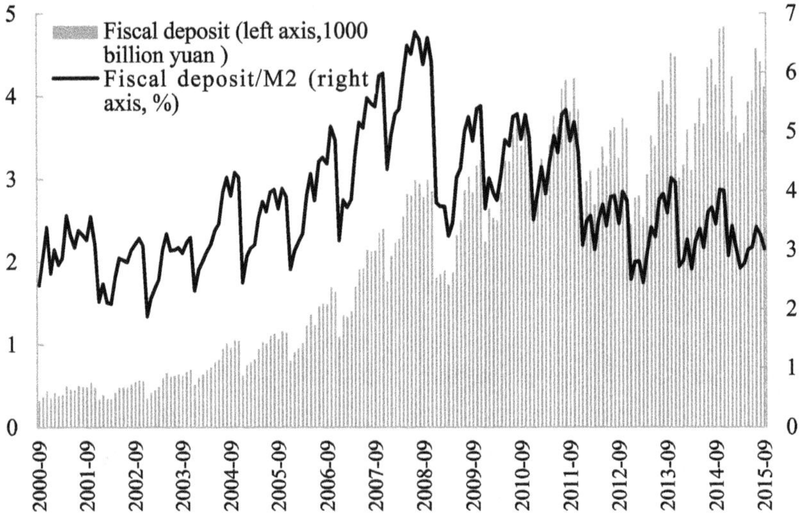

Figure 3-26 Fiscal deposit is still very high

2. While the conventional political - business relationship and interest community of government-private funds was shattered, new cooperation and mutual trust relationship had not been established. This lead to difficulties for governmental capital to initiate private capital in large scale. The stimulation effects of governmental investment and production declined substantially.

The relationship between entrepreneur and government, particularly private entrepreneurs and government, became more and more distant. The local governments not only became did not engine and locomotive of local economic development, but also became burden for local economy because of a large amount of arrears owed to small and medium enterprises. Many enterprises would rather do without orders than have a close relationship with governmental projects. This resulted in difficulties for PPP model promotion. It was hard for local infrastructure projects to carry out in traditional model. Many private entrepreneurs were less willing to invest under the mental pressure from "original sin". The outflow of capitals are increasingly severe. One obvious demonstration was that it became substantially less efficient for governmental funds to mobilize social funds into asset investment. From January to October of 2015, the cumulative efficient rate was 3.4 times, 0.8 time and 1.1 time lower respectively than the same periods in 2014 and 2013, and 1.5 times and 2.2 times lower respectively than 2012 and 2011. This indicated that stimulation effects of governmental investment and production substantionally declined.

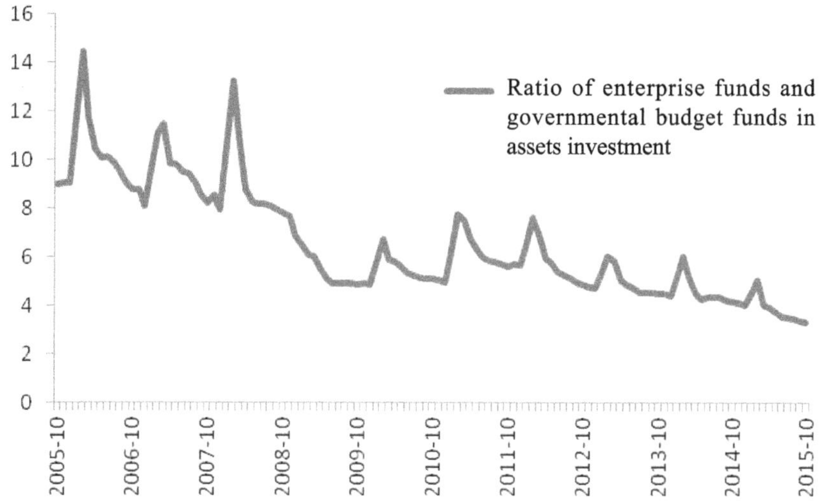

Figure 3-27 Stimulation effects of governmental investment and production went down dramatically

3. Scientific researchers was plagued by current financial inspection and reimbursement regulations, which made a large number of senior researchers and intellectuals do not want to undertake research projects. This lead to the fact that a large amount of research funds remained intact and was withdrew by the finance ministry in the end. This was specifically reflected in the following two aspects:

First, the saving of government organs and social groups was increasing rapidly. In September of 2015, the saving of government organs and social groups was 20930 billion yuan, 14.17% higher than the same period in 2014. The ratio of saving of government organs and social groups and M2 also constantly increased, reaching 15.39% in

September of 2015, 0.14% higher than the same period in 2014. One of the most reasons was tighter financial inspection making research funds appropriation and utility slower than expected.

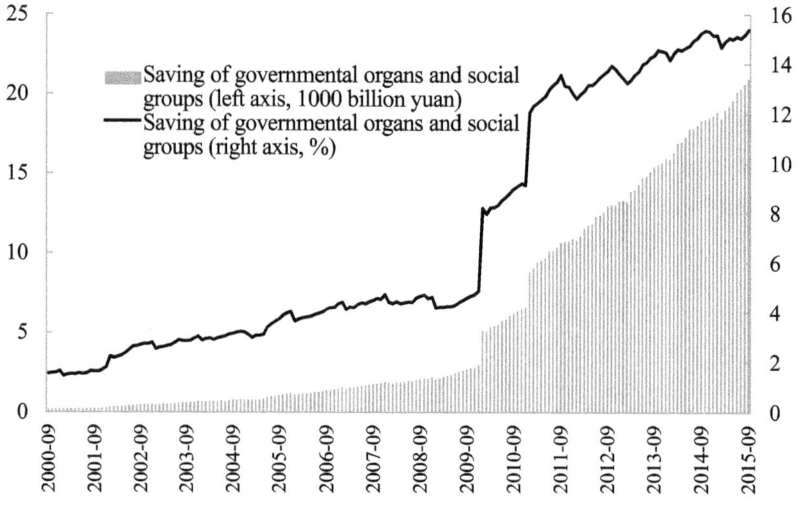

Figure 3-28 Saving of governmental organs and social groups was on the rise

To start with, the growth rate of university research expenditure declined substantially. In 2014, the growth rate of university research expenditure was only 4.8%, 5.0% lower than 2013, 15.2% lower than the average growth rate of the years from 2008 to 2012.

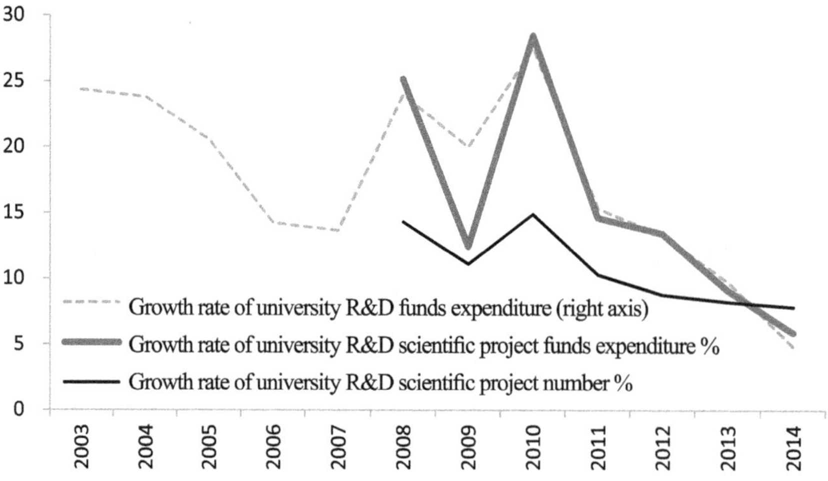

Figure 3-29 Significant decrease of university R&D funds

Secondly, the number of acceptance and licensing for patent applications experienced substantial decline, particularly for those patents which was able to reflect general situation of research findings. In 2014, the ratio of patent acceptance was 12%, 6 % lower than 2013, and 18.8% lower than the growth rate of the years from 2008 to 2012. In 2014, the growth rate of patent licensing in universities was only 0.1%, 13.8% lower than 2013, and 39.5% lower than the years from 2008 to 2012. In addition, the number of scientific papers published by universities also experienced dramatic decrease. The average growth rate from 2013 to 2014 was only 1.5%, significantly lower than the growth rate of 4.3 % from 2008 to 2012. among them, scientific papers published on overseas journals experienced larger decline with the average growth rate of 11% from 2013 to 2014, which was significantly lower than the growth rate of 16% from 2008 to 2012.

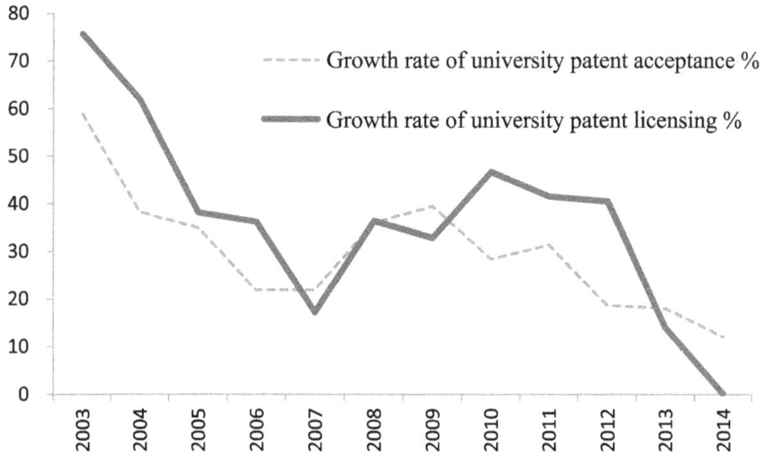

Figure 3-30 Growth rate of university research findings experienced sharp decline

Therefore, slackness of elites at all levels has become one of the most important reasons accounting for economic downturn. Practices of 30 years since the start of reform and opening-up and existing theoretical research findings indicates that if sustainable prosperity and economic growth of a country are decided not by technical, global, industrial or demographic dividends, but by a incentive mechanism of interest compatibility which set a same target for both elites at all levels and economic growth and maximize the interest of all classes during the optimization of economic resource allocation. if China wants to get rid of the economic downward, it does not only need to actively adjust and re-orient macro-economic policies, but also need to build up a incentive mechanism of interest compatibility in a short term during reform, which could provoke initiation of elites at all levels and let it become the essential driving force for reform and transition in new era, with the CPC Central Committee as the core.

Therefore, to build up an incentive mechanism of interest compatibility in a timely manner is one of the key issues which China should pay close attention to and try to solve. We should arouse people's enthusiasm and create a new climate in which people have no fears or reluctance in doing things, and do things in a scientific way.

(2) The situation of real estate investment, particularly if there will be a pick-up for real-estate investment in the second quarter of 2016. How real estate market will be recovered determined the growth rate of Chinese economy in 2016. Although the sales had shown significant recovery, there might not be a smooth road for real estate market to reach its recovery. The process of recovery will not only take a time longer than imagined, but also the differentiation during weak recovery will trigger "siphon effect" which would compound regional difficulties and stir up systemic risks.

1. Recovery of real estate market will take longer time than imagined.

Since April of 2015, affected by a series of easing-oriented policies such as "new policy of 30th of March", the real estate sales showed a trend of recovery. The total sales and floor space sold all stopped to decline and began to rise up on a year-on-year basis. The cumulative growth rates were respectively 15.3% and 7.2% from January to August. Meanwhile, housing price in more and more cities began to recover. Since April, housing price nationwide started to rise on a month-on-month basis, and began to recover since August on a year-on-year basis. Individual cities experienced substantial housing price increase. Therefore, many people believe optimistically that real estate market would embrace a new round of recovery.

However, according to our analysis, the process in which real estate market recovers will not be smooth, and will take longer time than imagined. From the point of view of supply factors in real estate industry which are more relevant with economic growth, no matter it is real estate investment or number of newly launched construction and land purchase indicators, all of these showed that real estate market is still in a state of downward and far from recovery. First, the growth rate of real estate investment showed a trend of continuous decline, with 19.8% in 2013 going down to 10.5% in 2014. From January to September of 2015, the growth rate further went down to 2.6%, 0.9% lower than the time from January to August. second, the number of new starts showed a trend of shrinking, with the growth rate of new space floor decreasing from 13.5% in 2013 to minus 10.7% in 2014. From January to September of 2015, the growth rate further went down to 12.6%, 4.2% lower than the time from January to August. At last, from the point of view of land purchase indicator, developers' enthusiasm in investing into market outlook was seriously inadequate. The growth rate of area of land purchased decreased from 8.8% in 2013 to minus 14.0% in 2014. From January to September of 2015, the growth rate further went down to minus 33.8%, 1.7% higher than the time from January to August. The growth rate of land transaction amount decreased from 33.9% in 2013 to 1.0% in 2014. From January to September of 2015, the growth rate further went down to minus 27.5%, 2.9% higher than the time from January to August.

Real estate enterprises had to bear constant pressure from shortage of funds. Since 2014, the growth rate of available funds decreased from nearly 30% in 2013 to almost zero or even negative, particularly so for bank loans and self-raised funds.

In September 2015, the real estate climate index, the comprehensive reflection of the extent of industry prosperity of real estate in China, was 93.40, a decrease of 0.06 point compared to August, which falls into the interval of serious depression and faces with great difficulty in recovering forcefully in short term.

From all perspectives, the current real estate market is still fragile and weak, and the transmission from sales recovery to new construction and investment even lags more seriously than before. There are mainly three reasons for such situation. Firstly, different from the previous real estate cycle mainly influenced by the tight regulatory policy directed at market overheating, the current market sluggishness is mainly caused by over stock of real estate, which is quite different from the cycle in the past. According to our estimation, the current real estate stock is 2~3 times of its sales volume, which is significantly higher than the historical average; besides, with the disappearance of the demographic dividend in the future, the real estate stock will suffer from greater pressure. This is also the main reason for the "weak recovery" of the current real estate market, namely, "volume increases, price stabilizes, and investment dims". Real estate developers that face with heavy destocking pressure generally adopt the marketing strategy of "trade price for volume" and the development strategy of "steady retreat". In this case, the subsequent investment is difficult to follow up and can only play quite limited stimulating effect on economic growth. Secondly, "anti-corruption" inhibits the market demand on real estate and reduces the enthusiasm of the government to cooperate with the real estate developers. Thirdly, the reorganization of "shadow bank" and trust business exerts a great impact on funding of real estate enterprises; in particular, the small and medium real estate developers with difficulty in funding through bank loans are facing with serious financial pressure and liquidity risk. In fact, this is the risk release period when a large amount of real estate debt is due and payable, therefore it requires close attention.

Under reasonable assumptions, we simulated and analyzed the adjustment process of the real estate market and the result showed that this round of market adjustment would last for a few years and generate adverse influence on investment and economic growth in the initial period. For 2016, the gross fixed capital formation of real estate might fall by 57%, resulting in decrease of 0.51% of GDP growth rate.

2. The recovery of real estate market faces a risk of midway failure

This round of real estate market recovery will not only be longer than expected, but also has a great uncertainty, which may lead midway failure in the end. There are mainly two big risks. First, in the short term macro economy will face a cliff-like drop, which will result in a sharp decline in resident income expectations, causing panic market. The real estate market recovery will be short-lived, and will in turn further aggravate the economic downturn to a contraction. Second, intensified market fragmentation under the fragile recovery may induce severe "siphonic effect", which will not only lead to local bubble, but also aggravate difficulties in some areas and induce systemic risks.

We believe that in the short term, the first risk is not very likely to happen, by contrast, the second risk worth more vigilance. It is normal to recover in market fragmentation, but compared to previous rounds, this recovery has an unprecedented degree, which mainly caused by factors of supply and demand. In the aspect of supply, distribution of the real estate inventory is extremely imbalanced between cities and cause real estate markets in various regions have different reactions to the ""New Deal". In recent years, first of all, first-tier and second-tier cities have largely kept stable inventory levels; only in some areas demand exceeds supply. However, in third-tier and fourth-tier cities, severe oversupply is prevailing and inventory rises sharply. Secondly, since middle and small-sized real estate enterprises, unlike large real estate enterprises, can get loans from banks easily, the reorganization of "shadow banking" and fiduciary activities in recent years has more serious impact on the middle and small-sized real estate enterprises, making them face severe financial pressure and liquidity risk.

In the aspect of demand, firstly, population further concentrated to large and medium-sized cities with the liberalization of household registration system and improvement of urbanization quality, transferring investment-oriented and improvement-oriented housing demands to first-tier and second-tier cities and further aggravating real estate inventory pressure in third-tier and fourth-tier cities. Secondly, main buyers in first-tier and second-tier cities are medium and high income groups, so it can avoid risks to allocate property in first-tier cities when market uncertainty increases; while main buyers in third-tier and fourth-tier cities are migrant workers, whose employment and wage growth have been impacted seriously by macro economy downturn in recent years, influencing their housing demand severely.

Market fragmentation aggravating in the fragile recovery may induce strong "siphonic effect". First, a large number of real estate companies will re-layout their development strategies to accelerate various types of development fund flowing to first-tier and second-tier cities. Second, real estate markets in third and fourth-tier cities will be further depressed instead of recovering under the lead of recovery in first and second-tier cities. Third, large real estate enterprises will improve performance in nationwide layout adjustment, while small real estate development enterprises will face failures. Financial difficulty in some counties will be further aggravated and then trigger partial financial risks and social issues. Fourth, at the current situation of very tight capital chain and high enterprise debt ratio, local capital chain break or financial risk are very likely to cause overall problems. Thus, the intensified fragmentation in the fragile recovery has great changes.

(III) External economic environment changes, especially if the world economy will face a double dip in 2016. In 2016, low external demand worldwide made great pressure for China's export, which squeezed space for economic recovery in China directly, while volatility in the international financial market will aggravate vulnerability of China's economy. In external economic environment, especially, situation changes in emerging marketing economies worth attention.

1. External demand may bring high pressure to China's economic growth by influencing China's foreign trade. Influenced by weak external demand and other factors, China's value of foreign trade in 2015 declined sharply and for the first time, export and import had "double down" since 2009. From January to September in 2015, China's export amount and import amount decreased by 1.9% and 20.4% respectively, and at the same time, the price index of export commodity and import commodity was in a negative range with -3.5% and -15% respectively in August, which was the first time for export and import price index had "double down" since 2009. The two unsymmetrical "double down" reflect that the external demand is extremely weak. To realize medium and high speed growth, China's economy must rely more on domestic demand and stimulate its growth, and even lead global growth through its own growth.

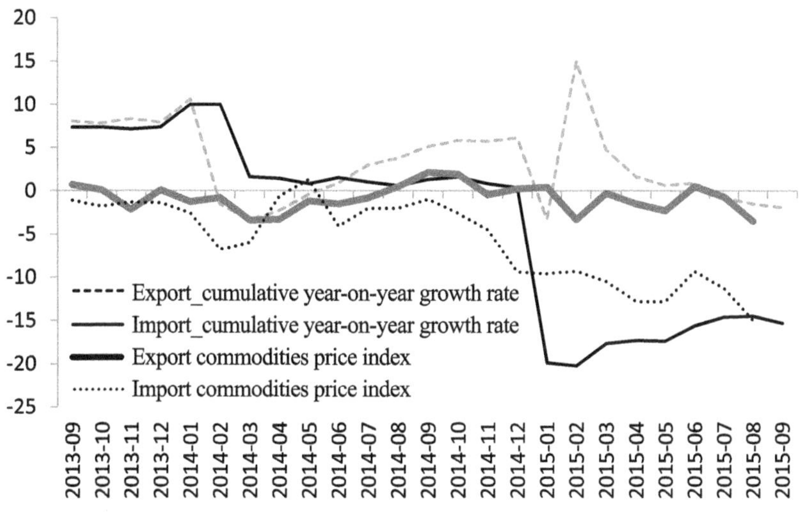

Figure 3-31 Weak external demand resulted in substantial decrease of China's foreign trade

From current expectation of international organizations and market, 2015 will be the end of this global economic cycle and the global economic growth and price level will rebound in 2016, which is conducive to China to realize its economy's bottom out. IMF predicted that global economic growth will be 3.6% in 2016, which is higher than 3.1% predicted in 2015 and 3.4%, the actual growth in 2014; IMF predicted that global CPI will be 3.3%, which is also higher than 3.2% predicted in 2015, but lower than 3.5%, the actual growth in 2014. Seen from different groups, IMF's expectation of developed economies' economic growth and price had risen. Developed economies' economic growth in 2016 was predicted as 2.2%, higher than 2.0% predicted in 2015 and 1.8%, the actual growth in 2014. IMF predicted that growth of emerging markets and developing economies will be 4.5%, also higher than 4.0% predicted in 2015, but lower than 4.6%, the actual growth in 2014. In addition, the market comprehensively predicted that global economic growth in 2016 will be 3.4%, higher than 3.0% predicted in 2015 and equals to the actual growth in 2014; the market predicted that global CPI will be 3.2%, higher than 2.9% predicted in 2015, but lower than 3.5%, the actual growth in 2014.

2. It is predicted that price of commodity will still be low in 2016, which is in favor of Chinese economic growth as a whole. Because sufficient crude oil, the global economic slowdown and increase of Iran's oil exports after international sanctions in 2016, it is expected that global crude oil prices will remain low in 2016. Thus, Commodity Markets Outlook, issued by the World Bank in October 2015, lowered its expectations for price of oil and other commodities. The World Bank predicted that compared to 2014, energy prices of 2015 fell 43%, and non-energy commodity prices fell 14%; and in the next five years, global commodity prices will continue to decline. However, because price of commodity, like oil, fluctuated seriously in recent years, coupling with increase of unstable factors, such as geopolitical relationship and politics, it is possible that oil prices may rise significantly in the second half of 2016. If this situation occurs, the enormous cost impact brought by this situation to the Chinese economy will be far greater than the marginal revenue of boost inflation from it, which will aggravate operating difficulties of Chinese enterprises.

3. In external economic environment, it is particularly worth paying attention to situation change of emerging market economies in 2016. Emerging economy is one of the central supporting point of China's trade, accounting for 30% of total trade, therefore, its downturn will seriously affect China's exports.

Firstly, the turbulence in emerging market economies started to become the weakness of global economic development. According to predictions of UNCTAD and IMF, it will be the low growth in emerging economies from 2015 to 2016, which will fall 0.5 to 1.0 percentage points compared to growth rate of 2014. Besides, it will be the immediate cause of deterioration in emerging economy trade from 2015 to 2016. According to current theory, "trade overshoot" existed widely after crisis, and the fall after rise of the GDP growth rate will lead to the decline in trade growth rate by double. As one of the central supporting point of China trade, emerging economies account for more than 30% of total trade, therefore, its downturn will seriously affect China's exports.

Secondly, the fragility of emerging market economies remains high, corporate debt levels constantly improve and liquidity risks increase. According to "World Economic Outlook" and "Global Financial Stability

Report" of MF in October 2015, although the financial stability in advanced economies had improved, the fragility of emerging market economies still remains high, its risk preference declines, and its market liquidity risks increase. Several major emerging market economies still face in significant unbalance in domestic and decelerated growth.

Since global financial crisis in 2008, debt levels of emerging market economies have continued to rise. In response to the global financial crisis, many emerging market economies conducted credit expansion, and the continuous low interest rates of advanced economies in the United States, Europe, Japan and others also encouraged the debit and credit of emerging market economies companies. Debt levels of non-financial companies in emerging market economies increased from about 4 trillion dollars in 2004 to more than 18 trillion dollars in 2014, and its proportion of GDP has risen sharply by 26 percentage points. In different countries, since the financial crisis, companies in China, Turkey and Chile had the largest rising range in leverage ratio, which all increased more than 20 percentage points. Followed by companies in Brazil, India, Peru, Thailand, Mexico, and many other Asian and Latin American countries, their rising range in leverage ratio were also more than 10 percentage points.

Moreover, constitution of debt in emerging market economies has also changed, corporation bonds became the new investment hot spot and risk points. Although bank loan is still a major component of corporate debt, the proportion of corporation bonds continued to rise, reaching 17% in 2014, which was twice as high as that in a decade ago. Affected by global factors of low interest rates, advanced economy investors seeking for higher benefits and commodity prices in "post-crisis" period, although balance sheet of emerging markets companies were weaker, they can still issue bonds with a lower rate of return and longer term.

The increased loans causes the leverage ratio of private sectors of emerging economies to climb sharply; which is good for emerging economies to promote investment by lever and thus boost the faster economic growth, but also generates some risks; besides, under the influence of global factors, the foreign currency exposure enlarges continuously, which makes the emerging economies become more sensitive to tightening of global financial conditions and makes the emerging marketing economy more weak when facing with higher interest rate, US dollar appreciation and increasingly serious global risks. When this credit cycle enters into the late phase, the capital buffer of emerging marketing economy will be weaker, and the deterioration of asset quality and profitability of the enterprise will lead to the increase in bad loans. In the condition of price declining of bulk commodity and slowing economic growth, some sovereign bonds in emerging market will be exposed to the risk of losing investment rating.

In 2016, the unexpected interest rate increase by the Federal Reserve or other developed economies might lead to fierce fluctuation of the market in emerging economies at any time. Once the United States and other developed economies start to increase the interest rate, enterprises with heavy debts will bear even heavier debt cost. The devaluation of domestic currencies caused by increased interest rate of developed economies will also make it harder for enterprises of emerging market to repay the debts in foreign currency. The price decrease of bulk commodity will further intensify the difficulties encountered with by some countries with emerging market. As the emerging marketing economy is caught in growth downturn and market disruption, the pressure on the external economic environment of China will further increase.

IV. The appropriateness of macroeconomic management in the economic dip mainly lies in its effectiveness in changing pessimistic anticipations of minor entities, and dissolving the comprehensive manifestation of "the deflation-debt effect". Also, its rationale relies on whether it can start up large-scale inventory adjustments in China and efficiently cut the endogenous deflation mechanism. And its efficiency exists in whether it can curb recessionary bubbles of all kinds and prevent and control the expense of local risks.

The year 2016 witnesses the full swing of China's economic dip, which may break the social bottom line or bring about huge pain. Meanwhile, the year 2016 marks the beginning of the strategic implementation of the 13th Five-Year plan. So the macroeconomic management will not only determine the success of the recovery from the macro-economic dip in 2016 but also decide the mid-and long-term tendency of China's economy. Attention should be focused on the effectiveness of policies in the following three aspects.

1. The Bottom Management of the Macro-economy

The year 2016 will be one for China's economic dip to proceed in an all-round way. It will extend the basic logic of the critical stage of the New Normal in China, making macroeconomic indicators of various kinds continue to be on the downward trend. Additionally, endogenous deflation and weakness in external demands will spread and enterprise behaviors will probably take on big variations. In 2016, many hidden troubles in the labor force market will begin to reveal and break the social bottom line. First of all, due to the press of destocking in the upper stream of the real estate industry, in the short term, the driving force for employment in the construction industry will be contained. Second, industrial sectors are still suffering from the pain of transformation, still excluding labor forces which number at least 4 million to 5 million. The industrial and construction industries, previously as two leading engines in absorbing labor forces, now face the problem of being underpowered. Also, the service industry confronts the signs of a declining demand in employment. In particular, in the consumer services largely accounting for employment, the employment expansion cuts back sharply. Additionally, in quite a few enterprises particularly in state-owned enterprises, such hidden unemployment as disguised wage reduction and decreasing working hours, step by step manifests. The bottom line of maintaining employment in 2016 calculated in the nominal GDP, demonstrates that China's economic growth rate need still remain at over 6.7% in order to create 10 million jobs in cities and towns. It also clarifies that even if the economic growth rate is allowed under 7%, there is not much tolerable dipping space. Accordingly, the bottom management of the macro-economy in 2016 gains much significance.

The success of the bottom management of the macro-economy lies in cutting the endogenous deflation mechanism. This means that the successful management will rest with transition from prudent monetary and fiscal policies toward moderately easy ones, stabilizing the market expectations, breaking the vicious circle of debit and deflation and reversing pessimism caused by endogenous fall. The effect of implementing relevant policies will depend upon the following three key points.

First, can the loose macroscopic readjustment and control policies break the traditional tempo of minor and microscopic adjustments so as to reverse the market expectations in an all-round way. In the past two years, China's macroscopic readjustment and control in the manner of minor adjustments have failed to reach the expected goal, the core reason for which is that the market entities have not recognized the minor adjustments. So the minor adjustments have not changed the expected model, not to mention playing the role of stabilizing confidence and giving play to the role of the anchoring effect.

Second, can the monetary and fiscal policies grasp the short window period at present to raise the easing to a certain level, break down the vicious circle of "deflation-high debt in the production sector" and avoid entering the balance-sheet recession, instead of adding loosing afterwards and failing to play the role of guidance? In case of China stepping into the balance-sheet recession, the effect of China's macroscopic readjustment and control policies will fall off a cliff with China's economic recession, resulting in rising readjustment cost. Cases of Japan and other countries have fully proven that the traditional pattern of minor adjustments will probably lead us to miss the best moment of readjustment. For China's economy to get around the balance-sheet recession, we should not only comprehensively transform the direction of macroscopic readjustment and control, but also ensure that the easing of monetary and fiscal policies will reach a certain high level.

Third, can "greater financial regulation" and "market order construction" be adopted in support of easy monetary and credit policies for fear of further inducing "the flow of capital from the real economy to the virtual economy", resulting in the divergence of the real economy from the virtual economy and the emergence of recessionary bubbles? Remedying the defects of the financial market and recovering its capability in allocating resources are an important premise for implementing a moderately easy monetary policy, as well as a key precondition for executing big-move strategies of all kinds.

2. The prevention and Governance of Recessionary Bubbles

With accelerated "capital flow from the real economy to the virtual economy", "recessionary bubbles" of various kinds have come into being. Continuously accumulating and expanding financial risks will gradually become the triggering points of macroeconomic variations. Accordingly, recessionary bubbles acquiring intensive prevention and dissolution contain those in the bond market, the real estate market in the first-tier cities, the strategic emerging industries and fluctuations in the international capital market. Inappropriate manners in dealing with these bubbles will not well prevent and dissolve them but probably speed up their formation and explosion, deepen the fragility of the overall Chinese economy so as to further worsen China's macroeconomic situation. Special attention should be paid to strengthening "financial regulation" and "market order construction" to avoid further flow of capital from the real economy to the virtual economy and trigger "recessionary bubbles".

3. Initiating Inventory Adjustments

Now China's economy is faced with serious inventory problems such as overcapacity, real estate inventory and high public debt, having indeed posed threats to its mid-and long-term development. Inventory adjustments are the basis of incremental ones. Although newly-created increasing points by incremental reforms, to a certain degree, can withstand the economic downward pressure caused by inventory problems, China's reform won't succeed without solving inventory problems. Under the circumstance of high debt, moderately ease monetary and fiscal policies should be maintained. Meanwhile, quite a number of "zombie companies" should be phased out of the market. Also, enterprises with high debt should have their debt reconstructed, and banks and related companies should have their balance sheets substantially reconstructed. Currently, some large-scale state-owned enterprises, in particular those in the four major heavy loss-making industries such as steel, coal and nonferrous metal, and "zombie companies" given special protection by the local governments out of their concern about stability, hold the majority of credit resources in the newly-added social financing. At the same time, these companies default on lots of loans, having actually been "the black hole vacuuming money" of the whole society, and intensifying difficulties facing other more effective companies to have better performances. In this case, an easy monetary policy cannot effectively alleviate the financing problems facing many enterprises. On the contrary, they may provoke the capital flow from the real economy to the virtual economy and asset bubbles.

Besides, while striving to cultivate strategic emerging industries, we need to make great efforts to lift the traditional manufacturing industry out of their management dilemma so that our economy can achieve a “soft landing”, transformation and upgrading. Therefore, as for China’s economic situation at present, the core for China to step out of the dilemma is to adopt “a proactive fiscal policy, a moderately easy monetary policy and greater regulation” based on the inventory adjustments. The effective solution of these inventory problems holds the key to accomplishing a real rebound of China’s macro-economy.

4. Major Conclusions and Policy Suggestions

4.1. Review and outlook

Based upon the above analysis, 2015 was the first year when the Chinese economy entered the difficult New Normal. The significant decline in the growth rate of nominal GDP and the continued negativity of the GDP deflator in the first three quarters indicated that Chinese macro economy was close to the edge of depression, when lack of effective demand began to replace the trend of decline as the main contradiction of macro economy. With the further implementation of the policy of "steady growth" in the second quarter, Chinese macro economy partially bottomed out and began to rise in the third and fourth quarters after foreign trade recovered, real estate investment bottomed out and consumption slightly picked up. However, as the "deflation-debt effect" continued to ferment, the macro economy showed constantly enhancing endogenous contracting forces. Accompanied by continuing deleveraging and destocking, significant fiscal difficulties at grassroots level, reversal of BEF in some industries and enterprises, diminishing effect of "micro-stimulus" and other factors, it was hard for the policy of "steady growth" to fundamentally change the path of this round of "asymmetric W-shaped" cyclical adjustment. And under the continuing influence of the midyear stock market crash, a solid bottom may occur one to two quarters later than expected in this round of cycle. From the cyclical perspective, 2015 was not the second bottom of this round of "asymmetric W-shaped" cycle, because the global economic cycle and the Chinese real estate cycle, debt cycle, inventory cycle, new industry cultivation cycle and political economic cycle determine that a solid bottom won't occur until late 2016. The year 2016 will continue the bottoming process of the New Normal of the Chinese economy, where many indicators will gradually stabilize in the sustained downturn.

Different from other years, 2015 had profound adjustment in a variety of structural indicators in the overall weak environment and saw prosperity in provinces and cities with successful transformation and depression in those with stagnant transformation, production slump, bubbles alternating in the stock market, bond market and property market, and stagnation of traditional manufacturing industries and rise of new industries. These phenomena not only marked the beginning of a critical period of the profound adjustment of Chinese economic structure, a window period of comprehensive release of risk, and a critical period of the bottoming of economic growth, but also meant that the Chinese economy began to breed new life in the slump. There was hope in the difficult time. The foundation for the new round of rapid growth was laid in the constant exploration. After 2015-2016 of cultivation of new growth sources and motivation mechanisms, there will be a steady bottom of Chinese macro economy in late 2017, which will gradually step on the path of rapid, steady growth. In this process, Chinese macroeconomic policy must focus on such important aspects as follows:

4.2. Reorientation of macroeconomic policy

4.2.1

Great attention should be paid to the impacts on the Chinese economy of the world economy during the great stagnation and differentiation. It is necessary to make an in-depth study of the nature and law of the current round of world crisis and grasp the nature of Chinese economic adjustment and the possible ways. In fact, the reversal of imbalance of the world economy and changes in the basic parameters determine that the "complementation-styled" incremental and inventory adjustment on the supply side is the basic policy orientation in this round of crisis management, which should be supplemented by the management on the demand side, of which the core is to prevent heavy aggregate fall and outbreak of systemic risk as a result of fierce transition.

In the context of the end of uneven development of the world economy and the reversal of trade imbalance, the core of Chinese economic transition should be to raise the overall supply of non-tradable goods based on substantial inventory shrinkage of tradable goods. The primary driving force for this transition manifests as an increase in demand for non-tradable goods and a decrease in demand for tradable goods and continuing adjustment of the two's relative prices; it manifests as full exposure of all kinds of bubbles and distortions grounded on imbalance and shows emerging risks on the other hand. In view of this, the various reform policies and adjustment strategies to promote the adjustment of relative prices adopted by China are reasonable. The simple use of macroeconomic policy to fill in the gap in demand for tradable goods and suppress demand for non-tradable goods not only cannot adapt to the tide of global imbalance adjustment but also may bring more transition risks to trade goods producers during the leveraging process. The core of the global structural reform lies in the "complementation-styled" incremental and inventory adjustment on the supply side while the core of demand policy is to prevent endogenous collapse caused by excessive exogenous adjustment and to prevent systemic risk caused by excessive release of risk in the imbalance reversal, which is complementary.

The structural adjustment policy on the supply side requires profound destocking and de-capacity in the sector of tradable goods in terms of inventory adjustment, and a significant increase in investment and supply in the sector of non-tradable goods with regard to incremental adjustment, which manifests as the increase in supply of various types of service and cultivation of new strategic industries. In this adjustment, there may be many spillover effects particularly in the inventory exit which can lead to lack of overall demand and structural depression. The emergence of these phenomena requires the full launch of the demand-side management.

4.2.2

The recent "recessive surplus" suggests that in addition to full launch of the supply-side management and reform, there's a need to reorient the demand-side management policy and make it more active.

The phenomenon "recessive surplus" occurred in 2015. It describes a substantial rebound of trade surplus in the significant fall of import and export growth after rise. Such a phenomenon cannot reflect the improvement in external demand or the end of the global imbalance reversal. Instead, it marks the beginning of a new stage, that is, the arrival of the "double depression", showing obvious structural impacts and aggregate impacts brought about by the continuing decline in external demand. In the past four years, China has adopted the strategy to complement external demand with domestic demand by means of credit expansion. It not only failed to lead the economy out of the woods but even aggravated its structural distortion and accelerated the fall in domestic demand during the process of "credit-investment driven mode" replacing "export-investment driven mode". Consequently, the drop in import demand becomes far greater than that in export demand, and the spillover effects of the global economic crisis begin to appear in China.

As can be seen in the national income identity (S-I) + (T-G) = (X-M), the "double depression" manifests as lack of private investment demand at home and recessive trade surplus abroad. There are some solutions to this dilemma. The first is to enhance the consumption and reduce savings rate radically, but this requires a medium-term orientation. The second is structural investment promotion policies. While expanding investment in non-tradable goods, China should curb investment in traditional export-oriented sectors and those with overcapacity. This approach is, however, subject to two constraints: (a) how to make differentiated structural investments; (b) investment cost-reducing policy is still vital when there is a significant decline in expected returns. Third, fiscal policy is the key to changing the "recessive surplus" in the short term. It is necessary to launch comprehensive tax cuts and spending expansion policy to greatly enhance the size of the fiscal deficit. In this regard, the structural dimensions of the proactive fiscal policy are very important, such as which one to choose between investment orientation and consumption promotion, between welfare promotion and one-off transfer payment, or between credit alternation and safe assets supply and simple subsidies.

4.2.3

There should be strategic recognition that enthusiasm of all levels of elites is the key to the present and future economic transition and upgrade and that excessive decline and sustained recession becomes the biggest political and social risk in China. After a major strategic victory in the fight against corruption, there should be new incentive and motivation mechanism for a new round of shake-up on the basis of steady growth.

(1) Construct a new positive incentive system of "opening the front door" by use of discipline inspection and improvement of the rule of law, and build a new performance evaluation system and a new official income reward system for the New Normal, in order to form a new pattern for the new round of reform and opening up. (a) Pacify government officials and elites through "separation between the new and the old", "interim summary", "classification" and other measures, get the historical burden off their burden, and involve all those loyal to the Party in the reform and transition of the new stage. (b) Establish a new transparent income composition mechanism so that political elites have a decent income under the premise of eradicating gray income from all forms of corruption. (c) Construct a new positive incentive-based official performance evaluation system that fits in with the New Normal to prevent the possibility that the evaluation becomes empty and general when the Only GDP theory is eliminated. The indicator GDP is still the core of evaluation of the government and its officials. In the new stage of accelerating development of China, the GDP indicator system can be moderately extended: first, reinforce periodic evaluation; second, strengthen evaluation in the green and livelihood dimensions; third, emphasize evaluation in the reform and transformation in the transition stage of the New Normal. An important thing worth noting here is that these indicators should be explicit in case that government at all levels loses their sense of direction in the overgeneralization. (d) Establish a number of new model officials with the ability and courage to reform, and tell the essential differences in procedure and structure

between breaking conventions and breaking law in the reform innovation through the large-scale expansion of negative lists of all levels of parties to the reform, so that the new batch of reformers can innovate without being limited on the basis of a clear bottom line. (e) Go through all kinds of financial systems, particularly the financial expenditure system, moderately relax management of special funds, encourage innovation in patterns of expenditure by locals government, and substitute the fiscal expenditure efficiency evaluation for those evaluation rules that cannot adapt to the new situation. The financial rules incompatible with the new financial times not only cannot restrict the officials and fight against corruption but even can be a source of evil deeds. The key to "opening the front door" is to promptly correct the outdated financial criteria including various types of meetings, business travels and overtime work.

(2) There should be both long-term and short-terming planning for the establishment of a new relationship between the government and enterprises and between politics and commerce. (a) In the short term, measures should be taken to eliminate the "original sin" burden of entrepreneurs and the legitimacy of entrepreneur's income and private property rights should be fully recognized; (b) Clean up the debts owed by local governments and large state-owned enterprises to all levels of enterprises, so as to clarify the "capillary" of the Chinese economy; (c) Fully implement the reforms of state-owned enterprises and release appropriate space for all kinds of small and medium enterprises; (d) Establish a more transparent politics-commerce relationship to further prevent collusion between political power and big capital.

(3) It's essential to reshape the overall enthusiasm for innovation of scientific and technical workers, strengthen the cohesion of intellectuals to the Party, and open a new way for intellectuals to participate in the reform and state governance. (a) There's a need for vigorous reform of the income system for research workers, full recognition of the rationality and legitimacy of intellectuals having a high income by innovative work, and establishment of a real income system that fits in with the innovative society and that doesn't fetter productive research workers with conventional standards. (b) There's a need for vigorous reform of the current backward research project reimbursement system, great increase in the proportion of research fees, labor costs and human labor expenses,

establishment of an incentive systems that encourages research and innovation, and prevention of restricting innovative activities with rigid financial rules. The key to changing the current slackness of researchers lies in "opening the front door" of the financial reimbursement system. (c) There's a need to boldly involve intellectuals without historical burden, "original sin" burden and constraints of political interests in the new round of reform and the modernization of state governance, construct a "revolving door" with Chinese characteristics by building a new high-end think tank so that a large number of intellectuals with administrative ability and officials with administrative experience take the think tank as the core and establish a elite flow mechanism between the government and non-governmental organizations and thereby form a new situation of expert governance with the enthusiasm of intellectuals fully aroused. For any major reform, it's vital to arouse the enthusiasm and participation of intellectuals to succeed and create a new look.

(4) The year 2016 should take the opportunity of economic bottoming to review and evaluate the current reform, seek a breakthrough, and search reform schemes for a viable path for reform. On the basis of existing top-down design and development idea, we should pay attention to the following major problems: (a) The conflict between excessive differentiation in different regions and the unified planning of top-down design, so we need to give play to enthusiasm and innovation of grass-roots reform in different regions; (b) The conflict between step-by-step reform and reform fragmentation caused by all departments acting their own way requires integration of power; (c) The antinomy of bureaucracies and elites as the object and subject of reform underlines the combination of centralization and decentralization in reform.

4.2.4

Great importance should be attached to two risks and four core areas that confront China in 2016. On the one hand, it's important to use supply-side adjustment policy and demand management policy to prevent endogenous downturn and prevent overall variation of microscopic subject behavior. On the other hand, attention should be paid to all possible "recessive bubbles" on the basis of stricter supervision.

(1) Great importance needs to be attached to the endogenous contractionary effect caused by deflation and high debt in production areas. On the one hand, a proactive fiscal policy and a moderately loose monetary policy should be pursued to hedge against the impacts of a heavy price fall. On the other hand, measures including debt restructuring, debt replacement, financing structure transfer, lowering of interest, tax cuts and reduction of administrative costs should be taken to solve the problem of high corporate debt.

(2) It's practical to clarify the microscopic mechanism of economic operation, restore the market's self-clearing function, and create a modest profit by sweeping away "zombie companies", restructuring debt-ridden enterprises, and accelerating the exit of industries with overcapacity.

(3) Debt replacement, asset securitization, macro debt-to-equity swap by use of the stock market and aggressive cut of interest rates should be pursued in parallel.

(4) Considerate attention should be given to the deviation of Chinese macro economy from finance. There should be strategic recognition of the necessity to use the prosperous stock market and bond market to initiate the capital market reform. At the same time, there must be also awareness of the risks caused by market bubbles to Chinese macro economy. First, the macro-prudential policy must focus on monitoring changes in asset prices at such time points as the US interest rates raising day, real estate investment rebound point and implementation of registration system. Second, reform and transformation of listed companies should be adopted to mitigate the current bubbles, so that the "money bull" and "policy bull" turn into "reform bull" in a real sense. Third, there should be coordination among corporate bonds unloading, additional issuance and IPO.

(5) It's essential to further boost the development of new industries through differentiated policies and further promote entrepreneurship and innovation activities from the system and mechanism. In the meantime, lessons should be drawn from the previous failures in emerging industries and innovation activities. And it should be noted that the state strategy cannot be converted into a short-term administrative movement of department at all levels and new rent-seeking activities cannot be encouraged through state

subsidies and other modes. First, respect the laws of innovation and entrepreneurship and avoid movement-like government support. Second, take advantage of the power of capital market to identify risks in innovation and avoid one-off administrative subsidies. Third, build all kinds of social safety nets for a soft landing of those who have failed in innovation and entrepreneurship so as to avoid strong impacts on the economy and the society of the wave of failures that may arise after the movement-like innovation and entrepreneurship.

4.2.5

It's necessary to strengthen the targeted easing of a proactive fiscal policy on the basis of further expansion of the deficit.

(1) There's a need to further increase the deficit ratio and improve government spending ability by use of wider issuing of treasury bonds in order to overcome the difficult situation of the decline in government revenue caused by the fall in GDP growth and sluggishness of land market in 2016. It is suggested that the deficit ratio reach 3% with a total amount of 2 trillion. Considering the small capacity of local debt market and institutional imperfection, it's suggested to increase the level of the fiscal deficit, of which the core channel is to increase the central budget deficit ratio, and to further expand the displacement scale of local government bonds, of which the core is to break through the current "safe asset shortage" faced by financial market by increasing the supply of government bonds.

(2) Attention should be paid to local fiscal revenue collapse and particularly all kinds of livelihood issues caused by the sudden change of grassroots fiscal revenue. It is recommended to expand the scale of the fiscal stabilization fund and establish the grassroots fiscal assistance system for the transitional period.

(3) It's practical to transform structural tax cuts into aggregate tax cuts, especially for those industries with insufficient supply, strong innovation and vitality and great upgrade pressure. At the same time, the target of fiscal revenue should be moderately weakened in case that local governments may increase the burden on businesses through more taxes and other ways.

(4) It is urgent to launch new fiscal expenditure initiatives for the transitional period, change the current difficult situation with expenditure, and introduce a series of measures that adapt to "opening the front door" of the new era.

(5) Fiscal expenditure should shift its orientation from investment to livelihood, from subsidy to welfare. Besides, the government should pursue a proactive fiscal policy to accelerate the nationwide welfare system construction and adopt a targeted easing policy to promote the development of the pension industry, health industry and high-end services and release the related demand.

4.2.6

Monetary policy should be fully reconstructed in accordance with the requirements of the new era, for the old one is inadaptable to China's current tough time of "new normal" development.

(1) At the time when endogenous fall speeds up and external demands remain weak, monetary policy must shift its focus from "steady positioning" to "moderately loose", so as to steady market expectation and break the vicious cycle of "debt to deflation", thus overturning the pessimism in the current endogenous fall. In the meanwhile, we need to hold the philosophy of "desperate times call for desperate measures", positively making prospective studies on pilot regions and implementing strategies of various irregular monetary policies. Hence, monetary policy must shift its aims from traditional CPI and employment to the following aspects: (1) nominal GDP growth, employment quality and GDP deflator; (2) liquidity stabilizing and transactions of asset prices; (3) exchange rate expectations and arbitrary capital flows. Meanwhile, since there are serious leakages in the intermediary goal of traditional monetary policies including M2 in the process of restructuring and system changes, therefore mere attention to M2, volume of social finance, financial terms for small and medium-sized enterprises and weighted loan rate is not sufficient to maintain a stable economic system. Thus, it is essential for a full implementation of macro-prudential supervision to step in.

(2) For loose monetary policy, to fully reverse market expectations, it must break the traditional "fine-tuning" mode, and fully understand

that the core reason that China's "fine-tuning" monetary policy did not reach the preset target in the past two years is that "fine-tuning"is not recognized by the main market players, that it neither changed its preset pattern nor stabilized confidence and bring anchoring effect.

(3) Break the vicious cycle of "deflation to high debt" in production and avoid entering balance sheet recession. Monetary policy must seize the current short window period, easing itself to a certain level, rather than make adjustment afterwards, which could cause the loss of expectation guiding. Once China has stepped into the balance sheet recession stage, the efficiency of China's monetary policy will also experience tumbling decline, bringing huge adjustment cost. Cases in Japan and other countries have shown that the traditional mode of "fine-tuning" may hinder the government from intervening at the right time, therefore China should avoid balance sheet recession, and not only make a comprehensive transformation of monetary policy direction but also make sure the loose policy brings enough impact at one time.

(4) In controlling the excessive debt rise, the choice of monetary policy tool is very important. Price tool is more favorable for the adjustment of business with high debt, the simple quantitative easing still needs control. Therefore, the positioning of the current loose monetary policy should mainly apply the price tool based on quantitative tools focusing on liquidity.

(5) The rigidity and high level of long-end interest rates do not mean that short-end interest rate adjustment is invalid, neither does the decline in corporate lending mean the loose monetary policy is unnecessary. On the contrary, even in the context where long-end interests are rigid and financial resources' penetration effect into real economy declines, loose monetary policy is also essential and will remain a necessary tool to guide expectations, avoid excessive contraction, and collaborate with active financial policy.

(6) "Wide currency" and bubbles of the financial sector are likely to further induce the capital to get "off real to virtual", causing deviation between real and virtual economies and resulting in "recession bubble". Therefore, the loose monetary policy must be complemented by "strong financial supervision" and "market order construction". The ability to compensate and restore the financial market allocation of resources is an

important prerequisite for not only the implementation of the monetary policy, but also various "macro-control actions".

(7) In the high debt environment, the government not only needs to maintain a moderately loose monetary policy but also cleanse a large number of "zombie enterprises" and regroup the enterprises under high debts. More importantly, a substantial reconstruction needs to be carried out on the balance sheet of the bank and related enterprises. Adjustment of the stock is the basis of incremental adjustments, especially for China's current environment, "proactive fiscal policy+moderately easy monetary policy+strong regulatory" based on stock adjustment is still the magic key for us to get out of the dilemma.

(8) RMB exchange rate fluctuations and Chinese capital flight may be the key factor for inducing risks in China after the crash of stock market. Therefore, monetary policy must focus on stabilizing the RMB exchange rate, "moderately loose monetary policy+exchange rate stability+strong external macro-prudential regulation" is still the core to respond fluctuation risks in the next two or three quarters.

(9) The integration of monetary policy, macro-prudential supervision, microfinance supervision and other financial goals becomes more and more important, and the substantiation, integration, independence and power-orientation of monetary and financial authorities are also the prerequisite to make scientific monetary policy. China's current financial power system has difficulty in managing the current monetary and financial policy, thus it is proposed that "one bank and three commissions" should combine together.

(10) Systematic studies should be made on unconventional monetary policy and even the Chinese QE. China's future policy basket does not refuse to take unconventional macroeconomic policies.

(11) To make good use of the window period, the government needs the mix of "moderately loose monetary policy+strong regulation", needs monetary policy to actively cooperate with the implementation of directional easing fiscal policy and adhere to the principle of "financial policy digs trench, monetary policy drains".

4.2.7

The government should continue to promote financial reform, especially combination measures such as China's macro policy of "removing leverage" in the capital market reform, asset securitization and the reform of state-owned enterprises.

(1) Problems such as the excessive growth of stock market index and local regulatory loopholes should not be given much attention. Registration system reform and IPO should be rapidly promoted based on capital market prosperity, in order to effectively reduce China's macro economy overall leverage and system risk through the transformation from debt financing to equity financing.

(2) Asset securitization for nonfinancial institutions should be accelerated.

(3) As the supervision strength on shadow banking increases, the bond market merger and debt financing scale increase go in parallel, especially the expansion of treasury market and merger of corporate bonds are significant.

4.2.8

Adjust the current real estate regulation and control policy, change the simple and loose policy orientation, make classified management for different regions and different types of real estate enterprises, and prevent further market differentiation.On the one hand, prevent the formation of a new round of upsurge of real estate prices; on the other hand, prevent real estate collapse in three or four-tire cities with excessive amount of land.

(1) Carry out the supply-oriented policies in the first and second-tier cities, focus on strengthening land supplies and loan support, speed up the transformation from real estate sales to investment, and avoid lowering investment in real estate too sharply to fall into deflation chains. At the same time, make reasonable expectation guidings and control house prices in the first-tier cities to prevent formation of new bubbles out of excessive rise. Housing bubbles in first-tier cities will accelerate capital separation from the real economy, weakening the boosting effect

of market recovery on macro economy, while the high price is also an important factor restricting the real estate demand.

(2) For three or four tier cities, demand-oriented policies should be carried out to encourage real estate sales and enhance the toughness of the recovery. Digesting massive inventory is the important method for real estate dealers to make the rapid withdrawal of funds, effectively reduce financial costs and defuse financial risks, as well as the prerequisite for real estate market to "empty the cage for more birds" and to ensure the future investment return to the track of sustainable growth. Policy initiatives should focus on stimulating the real estate market demand and encouraging real estate business to expand sales. At the same time, properly strengthen support to the real estate market in three or four-tire cities. Some ultra-conventional policies can be introduced, such as increasing financial support to the county-level government, and even setting up special funds to encourage local governments to buy commercial houses for affordable housing use.

(3) Pay high attention to the debt risk of real estate enterprises, especially the liquidity risk of small and medium-sized real estate enterprises, modestly strengthening credit support to real estate market, providing necessary liquidity, so as to ensure that real estate industries merge and reorganize in an orderly manner.

(4) On the basis of monitoring the differentiation index, we should coordinate with the pace of urbanization reform, especially the that of primary regions where population flows in and out, so that population growth in third and fourth-tier cities can gradually digest and absorb some of the stocks.

4.2.9

As macro-economic readjustments expand, the pressure of economic downturn is likely to further increase, thus we must pay high attention to the changing employment situation, prevent and resolve risks in the labor market.

(1) Implement active macro-control policies, prevent excessive economic degradation of certain industries and regions and maintain the overall stability of the labor market. The labor market is currently at the

critical point of large pressure, and further economic downturn could lead to higher employment pressure and break the tolerance limit of the society, causing stagnation of labor transferring and climbing of the unemployment rate.

(2) Further open service industry, encourage market access and competition and promote sustainable development of the service industry. Rapid employment increasing in service industry in recent years has released the long-restrained room over the past ten years. We should strive forward to further open the market access of health care and education, creating more jobs and helping increase economic profits and people's income. When carrying out those policies, we can improve the technical management standard of the industry by lowering requirements for administration access, so as to promote market competition and strengthen supervision.

(3) Pay attention to the developing continuity of traditional manufacturing industries and its coordination with the expansion of service industries, and pay careful attention to when to get into industrial transformation and upgrading and as well as when to get out. As China's labor cost increases, the transformation and upgrading of traditional manufacturing have become an irresistible trend, thus we should keep supporting technological transformation with more investments. However, since manufacturing is labor-intensive industry that plays the role of stabilizing employment during economic adjustment period, thus the transformation of traditional manufacturing should be carried out with its developing continuity maintained and in accordance with the particular development stage, rather than simply throw it all away. At the same time, relationship between the development of manufacturing and the expansion of the service industry should be well balanced. The employment situations in service industry and manufacturing are strongly supplementary, and as more and more industrial enterprises shut down or go broke, their supporting service industries are also going down. Thus, continuous deflation of manufacturing will certainly cause the unsustainable expansion of service industry.

(4) Special project should be introduced to further support the labor market flow under the circumstances that agricultural labor transferring is sharply slowing down. The project should include five aspects: first,

establish employment market sector for rural migrant workers, creating more job opportunities and increasing the flexibility of labor market; second, enhance training for migrant workers and improve their working skills and experience in urban areas; third, strengthen reform and implementation of pension transferring and renewing, promoting trans-border labor flow; four, improve migrant workers' social welfare in urban areas, including solving the education issue of their kids, thus increasing their motivation of transferring; five, facilitate the reform of household registration and rural land, eliminating barriers that hinder labor flow and accelerating urbanization. These measures not only help quicken labor transferring, but also enhance social security system and narrow urban-rural income gap.

This book is the result of a co-publication agreement between China Social Sciences Press (China) and Paths International Ltd (UK)

Chinese Macro-economy in the Process of Bottoming-Out and Rebounding
Authors: Liu Yuanchun, Yan Yan, Liu Xiaoguang
ISBN: 978-1-84464-508-4
Ebook ISBN: 978-1-84464-509-1

Paths International Ltd
PO Box 4083
Reading
United Kingdom
RG8 8ZN
www.pathsinternational.com

Published in the United Kingdom

CPSIA information can be obtained
at www.ICGtesting.com
Printed in the USA
LVHW020333070121
675928LV00003B/8

9 781844 645084